TÖILETRIVIA™

TRIVIA MIX

The only trivia book that caters to your everyday bathroom needs

by Jeremy Klaff & Harry Klaff

This book might contain product names, trademarks, or registered trademarks. All trademarks in this book are property of their respective owners. If used, they are for non-biased use, and we do not encourage or discourage use of said product or service. Any term suspected of being a trademark will be properly capitalized.

Cover art by Stephanie Strack

About the Authors

Harry Klaff covered the NHL for *The Hockey News* and *Hockey Pictorial*, and reported for both the Associated Press and United Press International. He has written three books, *All Time Greatest Super Bowl*, *All Time Greatest Stanley Cup*, and *Computer Literacy and Use.*

Today, he is a retired Social Studies teacher from Brooklyn. Because he never went on a date in his adolescence, Harry had plenty of time to research useless facts and figures on everything ranging from history to pop culture. Moonlighting as a hockey scoreboard operator and baseball beer vendor, Harry had ample time to collect data.

Yet somehow, he got married. In 1977, Jeremy was born. Rather than being raised on a steady diet of carrots and peas, baby Jeremy was forced to learn facts from textbooks. His first word was "Uzbekistan." Throughout his childhood, Jeremy had a hard time making friends. When other kids wanted to play baseball, he wanted to instruct them about Henry VIII's six wives. After a failed career as a standup comic and broadcaster, in 2000 Jeremy fittingly became a Social Studies teacher. Today he brings trivia to the next generation.

Collect All Toiletrivia Titles

US History

World History

Pop Culture

Sports

Baseball

Music

and more!

Get the full list of titles at www.toiletrivia.com

Acknowledgements

We at Toiletrivia would like to thank all of the people who made this possible.

- The ancient cities of Harappa and Mohenjo Daro for engineering advances in plumbing.
- Sir John Harrington for inventing the modern flush toilet.
- Seth Wheeler for his patent of perforated toilet paper.
- Jeffrey Gunderson for inventing the plunger.

We would like to thank our families for suffering through nights of endless trivia.

We would also like to thank the friendly commuters at the Grand Central Station restroom facility for field testing these editions.

Introduction

Here at *Toiletrivia* we do extensive research on what you, the bathroom user, wish to see in your reading material. Sure, there are plenty of fine books out there to pass the time, but none of them cater to your competitive needs. That's why *Toiletrivia* is here to provide captivating trivia that allows you to interact with fellow bathroom users.

Though most *Toiletrivia* volumes are on specified subjects, this version is a free-for-all, as questions are randomly mixed together on an array of topics. Each chapter allows you to keep score so you can evaluate your progress if you choose to go through the book multiple times. Or, you may wish to leave the book behind for others to play and keep score against you. Perhaps you just want to make it look like you are a genius, and leave a perfect scorecard for all to see. We hope you leave one in every bathroom of the house.

The rules of *Toiletrivia* are simple. Each chapter has 45 questions divided into three sections...One Roll, Two Rolls, or Three Rolls. The One Rolls are easiest and worth one point. Two Rolls are a bit harder and are worth two points. And of course, Three Rolls are the hardest, and are worth three points. You will tabulate your progress on the scorecard near the end of the book.

The questions we have selected are meant for dinner conversation, or impressing people you want to date. With few exceptions, our queries are geared for the uncomfortable situations that life throws at you, like when you have nothing in common with someone, and need to offer some clever banter. We hope that the facts you learn in the restroom make it easier to meet your future in-laws, or deal with that hairdresser who just won't stop talking to you.

Remember, *Toiletrivia* is a game. No joysticks, no computer keyboards...just you, your toilet, and a pen; the way nature intended it. So good luck. We hope you are triumphant.

DIRECTIONS

Each set of questions has an answer sheet opposite it. Write your answers in the first available column to the right. When you are done with a set of 15 questions, ***fold*** your answer column underneath so the next restroom user doesn't see your answers. *Special note to restroom users 2 and 3: No cheating! And the previous person's answers might be wrong!*

Then check your responses with the answer key in the back of the book. Mark your right answers with a check, and your wrong answers with an "x." Then go to the scorecard on pages 98-100 and tabulate your results. These totals will be the standard for other users to compare.

Table of Contents

Trivia Mix 1

Flip to pg. 68 for answers

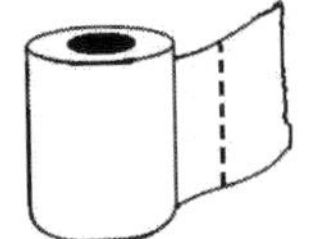

One Roll

1. What is the color of a Hershey's Krackel wrapper?
2. Who was the fattest President?
3. What popular steak sauce was created by a chef for King George IV?
4. What's the big island off the east coast of Africa?
5. Ironically, this legendary comedian recorded *Live & Smokin'* about a decade before he set himself on fire. Name him.
6. What kitchen staple is *origanum vaajdladn* better known as?
7. What has been the highest selling fiction book of the 21st century?
8. How many bagels are in a baker's dozen?
9. In what ocean would one find the greatest abundance of sockeye salmon?
10. What is the next prime number that follows 11, 13, 17, 19, and 23?
11. What was boxer Rocky Balboa's nickname?
12. What two dairy products are traditionally added to a box of macaroni and cheese?
13. What Pennsylvania city was home to *The Office*?
14. Atop Snoopy's doghouse, what sleepy bird would often be seen with a "z" coming out of his mouth?
15. Our galaxy has well over 100 billion stars in it. What's the name of our galaxy?

Answer Sheet Trivia Mix 1 1 Roll	Answer Sheet Trivia Mix 1 1 Roll	Answer Sheet Trivia Mix 1 1 Roll
Name________________	Name________________	Name________________
1.	1.	1.
2.	2.	2.
3.	3.	3.
4.	4.	4.
5.	5.	5.
6.	6.	6.
7.	7.	7.
8.	8.	8.
9.	9.	9.
10.	10.	10.
11.	11.	11.
12.	12.	12.
13.	13.	13.
14.	14.	14.
15.	15.	15.

After you have filled out the sheet, fold your column underneath along the dashed line so the next restroom user won't see your answers. ***The first player uses the far right column.***

Notes:	***Notes:***	***Notes:***

Trivia Mix 1

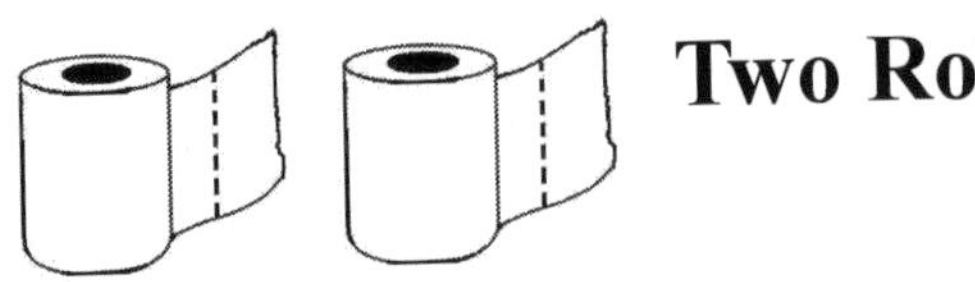

Two Rolls

1. "Shave and a haircut…two bits!" How much money was two bits worth?

2. How many *Friends* were there on the popular sitcom?

3. Often called butter beans, or chad beans, what vegetable is believed to have originated in Peru?

4. One of the most popular toys of all time was designed to clean wallpaper. Name that toy.

5. What mythical figure of the deep sea has been proven to exist in pictures…complete with tentacles?

6. Of the following items, which one did not exist in the Americas in 1491? Pineapple, horse, turkey, pumpkin.

7. In 2012, Adele tied the record for most Grammy Awards won by a female in one night. Whose record did she tie?

8. Mark Twain was born and died on days when what celestial object was visible?

9. Which is greater…the number of World Series won by the New York Yankees, the total of Olympic medals won by Michael Phelps, or the number of Stanley Cups won by the Montreal Canadiens?

10. What colony became "lost," failing to become the first permanent English settlement in North America?

11. Who is Superman's biological father?

12. Lorraine Hansberry's title, *A Raisin in the Sun*, was inspired by a poem from what Harlem Renaissance poet?

13. What insect returned to North America to complete its 17 year lifecycle in 2013?

14. What does ROTC stand for?

15. What color is a bag of original Funyuns Onion Flavored Rings?

Answer Sheet	**Answer Sheet**	**Answer Sheet**
Trivia Mix 1 **2 Rolls**	**Trivia Mix 1** **2 Rolls**	**Trivia Mix 1** **2 Rolls**
Name________________	**Name**________________	**Name**________________
1.	1.	1.
2.	2.	2.
3.	3.	3.
4.	4.	4.
5.	5.	5.
6.	6.	6.
7.	7.	7.
8.	8.	8.
9.	9.	9.
10.	10.	10.
11.	11.	11.
12.	12.	12.
13.	13.	13.
14.	14.	14.
15.	15.	15.

After you have filled out the sheet, fold your column underneath along the dashed line so the next restroom user won't see your answers. ***The first player uses the far right column.***

Notes:	***Notes:***	***Notes:***

Trivia Mix 1

Flip to pg. 70 for answers

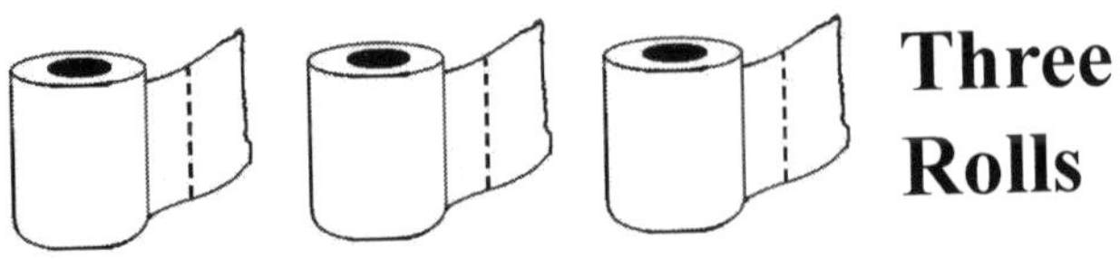

1. What is the more scientific name for “eye crust”?

2. Who wrote *Fifty Shades of Grey*?

3. After Mandarin, what is the most widely spoken language native to Asia?

4. What is the real name of the Boston bar whose exterior is seen on the sitcom *Cheers*?

5. What Los Angeles Rams defensive end was credited with coining the term “sack”?

6. Dating back to 1990, what is widely considered to be the first web search engine? It has the same name as a comic.

7. For over thirty years, what Minnesota-based company’s product has helped teachers accurately score multiple choice questions at a rapid rate?

8. What Shakespearean play, written entirely in verse, is the first of the *Henriad*?

9. Alaska (1959) and Hawaii (1959) were the last two states admitted to the 50 United States. Which state became Number 48 in 1912?

10. *A Man, A Plan, A Canal: Panama* spelled backwards is *A Man, A Plan, A Canal: Panama*. What do we call such words or phrases like this?

11. What name is given to lines on a weather map that connect areas of equal atmospheric pressure?

12. Before it was *Pac-Man*, what was the name of the iconic video game? Hint: The title was changed to prevent graffiti to its name in the arcade.

13. What 1970s purple cartoon gorilla frequently repeated his name?

14. What is the deepest point of the ocean?

15. Name three of the four NBA teams that don’t end in the letter “S.”

Answer Sheet Trivia Mix 1 3 Rolls	**Answer Sheet** Trivia Mix 1 3 Rolls	**Answer Sheet** Trivia Mix 1 3 Rolls
Name________________	**Name**________________	**Name**________________
1.	1.	1.
2.	2.	2.
3.	3.	3.
4.	4.	4.
5.	5.	5.
6.	6.	6.
7.	7.	7.
8.	8.	8.
9.	9.	9.
10.	10.	10.
11.	11.	11.
12.	12.	12.
13.	13.	13.
14.	14.	14.
15.	15.	15.

After you have filled out the sheet, fold your column underneath along the dashed line so the next restroom user won't see your answers. ***The first player uses the far right column.***

Notes:	***Notes:***	***Notes:***

Trivia Mix 2

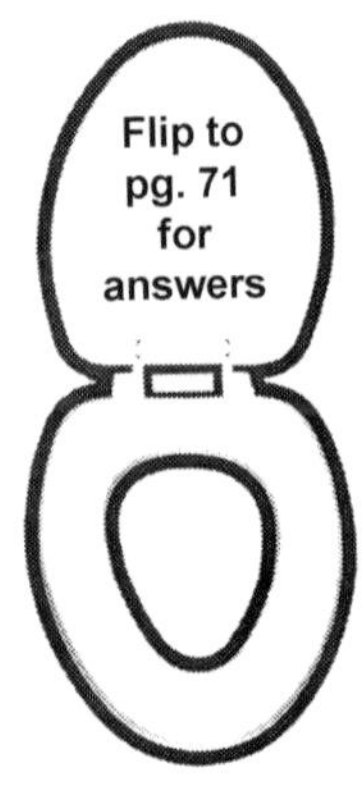

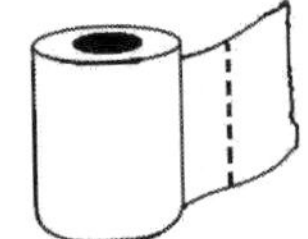

One Roll

1. Here's a toss-up: Does a set of XY chromosomes mean a baby will be male or female?

2. On what television show would one have found Carlton Banks?

3. What two colors are on Fred Flintstone's shirt?

4. In golf, what word is commonly used for a 1-wood?

5. What was the first movie in the *Indiana Jones* series?

6. What Bay Area valley is known for its wine?

7. "Densely," "greatly," and "suddenly," are all examples of what type of words?

8. What tiny pickles are usually just a couple of inches in length?

9. What does the SVU stand for in *Law & Order: SVU*?

10. In 1989, what electronics giant changed its logo and put it on a yellow price tag?

11. What star is 93 million miles away from Earth?

12. Who is Dora the Explorer's cousin? He would receive his own spin-off.

13. Who was lurking one story above Abraham Lincoln as he delivered his second inaugural address?

14. Pamplona's "encierro" is better known to the world as what event?

15. What type of shirt looks like the letter it's named for when it's unfolded?

Answer Sheet Trivia Mix 2 1 Roll	Answer Sheet Trivia Mix 2 1 Roll	Answer Sheet Trivia Mix 2 1 Roll
Name______	Name______	Name______
1.	1.	1.
2.	2.	2.
3.	3.	3.
4.	4.	4.
5.	5.	5.
6.	6.	6.
7.	7.	7.
8.	8.	8.
9.	9.	9.
10.	10.	10.
11.	11.	11.
12.	12.	12.
13.	13.	13.
14.	14.	14.
15.	15.	15.

After you have filled out the sheet, fold your column underneath along the dashed line so the next restroom user won't see your answers. ***The first player uses the far right column.***

Notes:	***Notes:***	***Notes:***

Trivia Mix 2

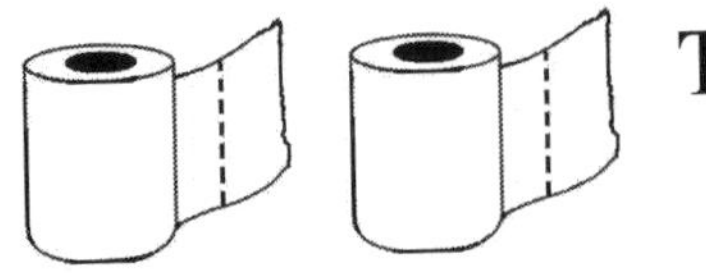

Two Rolls

1. What language is comprised of a variety of tongues including Hebrew and German?

2. What comedian hosted the fictitious *The Larry Sanders Show*?

3. What is the highest grossing superhero movie of all time?

4. How long is a fortnight?

5. What continent is home to the alpaca?

6. What breed of dog is traditionally used in track races?

7. What newswoman became Howard Stern's sidekick?

8. What element is Ag on the periodic table?

9. How many notes are in *Taps*?

10. What neutral force protects Vatican City?

11. What country in the world has the most cities that begin with the letter X?

12. How many candles are in a Kwanzaa kinara?

13. What are the three main ingredients in a Nestlé Chunky bar?

14. What town in New York was established by writer James Fenimore Cooper's father?

15. If a person is gregarious, how do they act?

Answer Sheet Trivia Mix 2 2 Rolls	**Answer Sheet** Trivia Mix 2 2 Rolls	**Answer Sheet** Trivia Mix 2 2 Rolls
Name________________	**Name**________________	**Name**________________
1.	1.	1.
2.	2.	2.
3.	3.	3.
4.	4.	4.
5.	5.	5.
6.	6.	6.
7.	7.	7.
8.	8.	8.
9.	9.	9.
10.	10.	10.
11.	11.	11.
12.	12.	12.
13.	13.	13.
14.	14.	14.
15.	15.	15.

After you have filled out the sheet, fold your column underneath along the dashed line so the next restroom user won't see your answers. ***The first player uses the far right column.***

Notes:	***Notes:***	***Notes:***

Trivia Mix 2

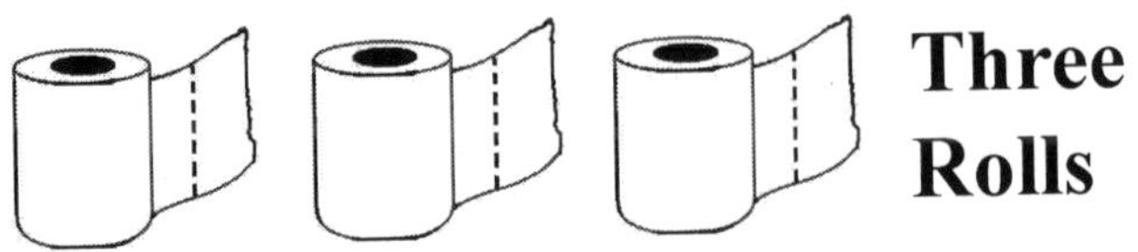

Three Rolls

1. How many flavors are in the patented formula of Dr. Pepper?

2. What is the easternmost Canadian province?

3. Who are Miranda rights named after? (First name please)

4. What was the first Major League Baseball ballpark to host a night game under the lights?

5. In 1914, who assassinated Archduke Franz Ferdinand to trigger World War I?

6. In web programming, what does FTP stand for?

7. Within one day, how long is a Lunar Month?

8. What is the name of the dot that goes above a lowercase i or j?

9. Who is the protagonist in the video game, *The Legend of Zelda*?

10. What fruit, often considered a vegetable, is also known as the Alligator Pear?

11. According to legend, who ran about 26 miles to ancient Athens to announce a military victory, and thus unintentionally invented the Marathon?

12. What company was the first to trademark a breakfast cereal way back in 1877?

13. What male music artist's CD was the first to be manufactured in the United States? The album's title is quite fitting for this question.

14. What form of a verb acts like an adjective when modifying a noun?

15. What ancient Greek stadiums typically hosted chariot races? Starts with H.

Answer Sheet	Answer Sheet	Answer Sheet
Trivia Mix 2 3 Rolls	Trivia Mix 2 3 Rolls	Trivia Mix 2 3 Rolls
Name________________	Name________________	Name________________
1.	1.	1.
2.	2.	2.
3.	3.	3.
4.	4.	4.
5.	5.	5.
6.	6.	6.
7.	7.	7.
8.	8.	8.
9.	9.	9.
10.	10.	10.
11.	11.	11.
12.	12.	12.
13.	13.	13.
14.	14.	14.
15.	15.	15.

After you have filled out the sheet, fold your column underneath along the dashed line so the next restroom user won't see your answers. ***The first player uses the far right column.***

Notes:	***Notes:***	***Notes:***

Trivia Mix 3

Flip to pg. 74 for answers

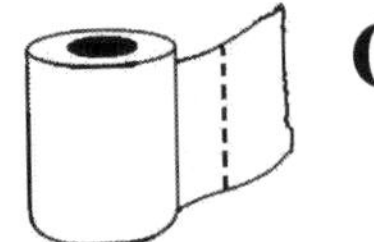

One Roll

1. What plastic or metallic coil toy can "walk" down the stairs?

2. What heroine's alter-ego is Princess Diana of Themyscira?

3. Which early First Lady became associated with ice cream?

4. What is the Spanish word for pants?

5. Name the two American comedians who died exactly at the age of 100 ...one in 1996 and the other in 2003.

6. Which type of lettuce is traditionally served in a Caesar Salad?

7. What Japanese term refers to a gigantic wave that's triggered by an ocean disturbance, such as an earthquake?

8. What type of animal is the mascot for Aflac Incorporated?

9. Name the US National Park which is home to Half Dome and El Capitan.

10. Identify the chemical formula for table salt.

11. What is the device that raises and lowers boats in a canal?

12. By far, what is the highest selling book (fiction or nonfiction) of all time?

13. New Kids on the Block, 'N Sync, and the Backstreet Boys were all assembled with the same amount of members. How many?

14. What type of vehicle is Autobot leader Optimus Prime of the *Transformers*?

15. What company launched a new line of disposable pens in 1950?

Answer Sheet **Trivia Mix 3** **1 Roll** **Name**______________	**Answer Sheet** **Trivia Mix 3** **1 Roll** **Name**______________	**Answer Sheet** **Trivia Mix 3** **1 Roll** **Name**______________
1.	1.	1.
2.	2.	2.
3.	3.	3.
4.	4.	4.
5.	5.	5.
6.	6.	6.
7.	7.	7.
8.	8.	8.
9.	9.	9.
10.	10.	10.
11.	11.	11.
12.	12.	12.
13.	13.	13.
14.	14.	14.
15.	15.	15.

After you have filled out the sheet, fold your column underneath along the dashed line so the next restroom user won't see your answers. ***The first player uses the far right column.***

Notes:

Notes:

Notes:

Trivia Mix 3

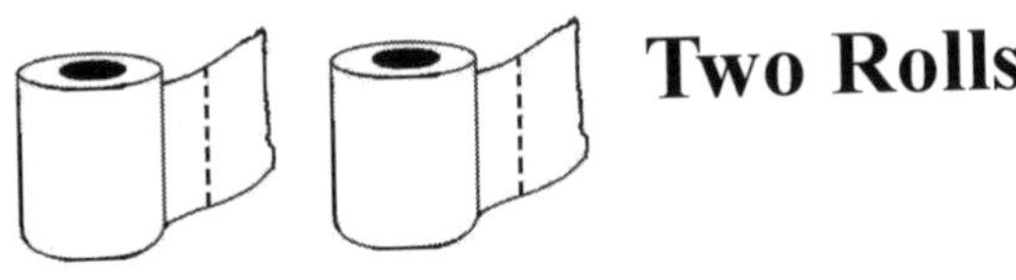

Two Rolls

1. Which Brontë wrote *Jane Eyre*?
2. In what modern-day country did the language Farsi develop?
3. How many laces are on a football?
4. Who was the first female prime minister of Israel?
5. In his book, *God in Popular Culture*, who did author Andrew Greeley believe to be the most successful female rock star of the 1970s? If you get this wrong, *You're no Good.*
6. What children's song's verse can be translated to, "are you sleeping, Brother (or Friar) John"?
7. What Fruit of the Loom children's favorite features superhero characters on underwear?
8. What term refers to large clouds of gas and dust that can lead to the creation of stars?
9. Within 3, how many electoral votes did California have in the 2012 election?
10. By the early nineteenth century, what did cotton replace as the major cash crop of the southern United States?
11. What cooling agent is nothing more than solid carbon dioxide?
12. What intense slogan is on the New Hampshire license plate?
13. What Russian monarch collected bizarre items, including human skeletons, hearts, and pickled heads?
14. According to the owl in the classic commercial, how many licks does it take to get to the center of a Tootsie Pop?
15. What is the only US state to grow massive amounts of coffee?

Answer Sheet

Trivia Mix 3
2 Rolls

Name________________

1.
2.
3.
4.
5.
6.
7.
8.
9.
10.
11.
12.
13.
14.
15.

Answer Sheet

Trivia Mix 3
2 Rolls

Name________________

1.
2.
3.
4.
5.
6.
7.
8.
9.
10.
11.
12.
13.
14.
15.

Answer Sheet

Trivia Mix 3
2 Rolls

Name________________

1.
2.
3.
4.
5.
6.
7.
8.
9.
10.
11.
12.
13.
14.
15.

After you have filled out the sheet, fold your column underneath along the dashed line so the next restroom user won't see your answers. ***The first player uses the far right column.***

Notes:

Notes:

Notes:

Trivia Mix 3

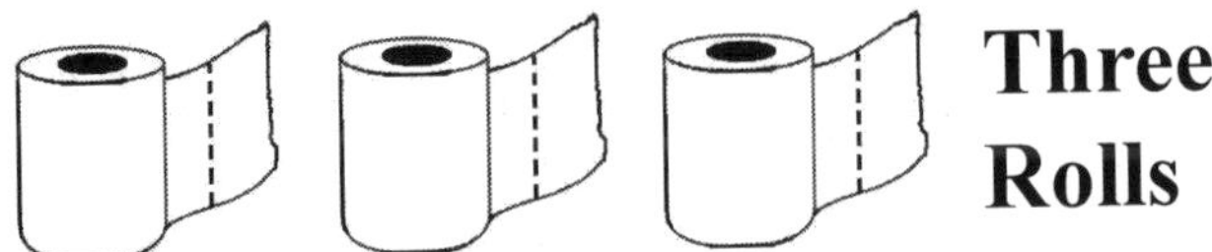

Three Rolls

1. During which epoch did the last Ice Age occur?
2. What is the atomic number of Oxygen?
3. What fruit is named for Australian Maria Ann Smith, the woman who popularized it?
4. Within 5, how many people signed the Declaration of Independence?
5. What does someone with *Ophidiophobia* fear?
6. What does DNA stand for?
7. In 2012, Miguel Cabrera of the Detroit Tigers became the first player in decades to win the American League Triple Crown. Who last accomplished this achievement in 1967?
8. What country did East Pakistan become in 1971?
9. What is the currency called in Uganda, Somalia, and Tanzania?
10. According to Baskin-Robbins, what are their top five selling ice cream flavors? (Name 3 for the points.)
11. What was Cher's birth name?
12. What is the name of the telescope lens which will increase the magnification of the other eyepiece you are using?
13. In what year were quarterbacks John Elway, Jim Kelly, and Dan Marino all drafted?
14. What was the most popular baby boy name in the United States for 2012? Starts with J.
15. What seventeenth century Spanish novel is accepted to be the highest-selling fictional work of all time?

Answer Sheet Trivia Mix 3 3 Rolls	Answer Sheet Trivia Mix 3 3 Rolls	Answer Sheet Trivia Mix 3 3 Rolls
Name__________	Name__________	Name__________
1.	1.	1.
2.	2.	2.
3.	3.	3.
4.	4.	4.
5.	5.	5.
6.	6.	6.
7.	7.	7.
8.	8.	8.
9.	9.	9.
10.	10.	10.
11.	11.	11.
12.	12.	12.
13.	13.	13.
14.	14.	14.
15.	15.	15.

After you have filled out the sheet, fold your column underneath along the dashed line so the next restroom user won't see your answers. ***The first player uses the far right column.***

Notes:	*Notes:*	*Notes:*

Trivia Mix 4

Flip to pg. 77 for answers

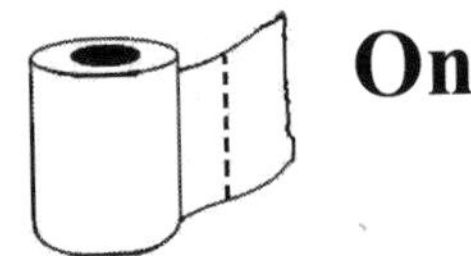

One Roll

1. What actor was *Driving Miss Daisy*?

2. What President was nicknamed "Old Hickory"?

3. Which country was the backdrop for *The Kite Runner*?

4. What tasty monarch is on the top of the *Candy Land* board?

5. What two numbers on a modern telephone have four letters above them instead of three?

6. Whose hit, *Saving All My Love for You*, was one of three songs to top the *Billboard* Hot 100 chart within a one year span? All three hits came off of her 1985 self-titled album.

7. What actor stood in Hilary Swank's corner in the hit movie, *Million Dollar Baby*?

8. What is Peru's most visited tourist attraction?

9. Just by looking at their ears, how can you tell the difference between an Asian elephant and an African one?

10. Toss-up: Is orzo rice or pasta?

11. With its advanced cryogenic freezing process, what frozen treat is deemed "the ice cream of the future"?

12. What popular board game was first called *Lexiko* and then *Criss-Cross Words*?

13. What is the name of the skin which holds sausages together?

14. What ground-breaking reality show first took place off the coast of Borneo in 2000?

15. Who is Dwayne Johnson's wrestling alter-ego?

Answer Sheet **Trivia Mix 4** **1 Roll** **Name**____________	**Answer Sheet** **Trivia Mix 4** **1 Roll** **Name**____________	**Answer Sheet** **Trivia Mix 4** **1 Roll** **Name**____________
1.	1.	1.
2.	2.	2.
3.	3.	3.
4.	4.	4.
5.	5.	5.
6.	6.	6.
7.	7.	7.
8.	8.	8.
9.	9.	9.
10.	10.	10.
11.	11.	11.
12.	12.	12.
13.	13.	13.
14.	14.	14.
15.	15.	15.

After you have filled out the sheet, fold your column underneath along the dashed line so the next restroom user won't see your answers. ***The first player uses the far right column.***

Notes:

Notes:

Notes:

Trivia Mix 4

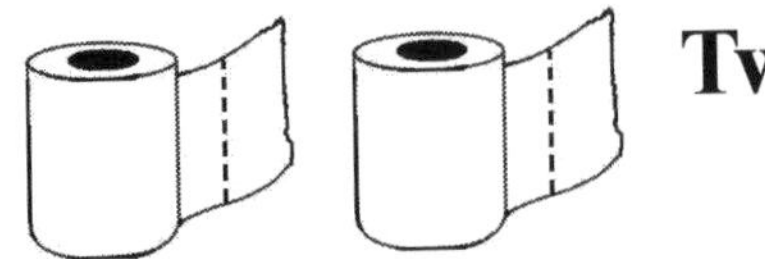

Two Rolls

1. In 2013, all of the Baseball Hall of Fame inductees had something in common not shared since 1965. What was it?

2. No peeking in a mirror! Within 2, how many teeth are in a normal human mouth?

3. In bowling, what is a “turkey”?

4. What notorious 1930s bank-robber wound up as a pitchman in a 1970s bank commercial?

5. The type of grass one would find on most south Florida lawns has the same name as the oldest city in the United States. What is it?

6. Meaning “spouting fresh water” in Hawaiian, what famous beach is on the southern shore of Oahu?

7. What does EA stand for, as in the EA Sports company that turns out video game hits such as *Madden NFL*?

8. Which Founding Father has been given credit for introducing “potatoes, served in the French manor” to the United States?

9. What city is home to the Blue Mosque (Sultan Ahmet Camii)?

10. Of *Star Wars*, *The Lord of the Rings*, and *Harry Potter*, which series claims the most movies?

11. What are the two levels of a fraction called?

12. In 1992, who played The Penguin in *Batman Returns*?

13. Of Bill Russell, Kareem Abdul-Jabbar, Shaquille O’Neal, Kobe Bryant, and Wilt Chamberlain, who won the most NBA Championships?

14. What number on a keyboard has a $ above it?

15. What title was World War I pilot Manfred von Richthofen more commonly known as?

Answer Sheet

Trivia Mix 4
2 Rolls

Name________________

1.
2.
3.
4.
5.
6.
7.
8.
9.
10.
11.
12.
13.
14.
15.

Answer Sheet

Trivia Mix 4
2 Rolls

Name________________

1.
2.
3.
4.
5.
6.
7.
8.
9.
10.
11.
12.
13.
14.
15.

Answer Sheet

Trivia Mix 4
2 Rolls

Name________________

1.
2.
3.
4.
5.
6.
7.
8.
9.
10.
11.
12.
13.
14.
15.

After you have filled out the sheet, fold your column underneath along the dashed line so the next restroom user won't see your answers. ***The first player uses the far right column.***

Notes:

Notes:

Notes:

Trivia Mix 4

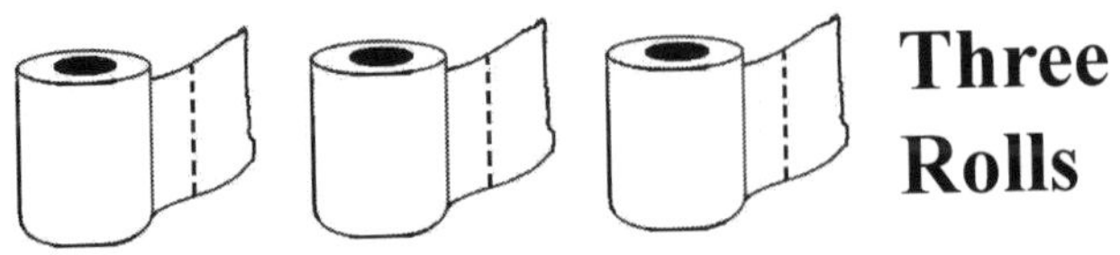

Three Rolls

1. What are the two photoreceptors of the retina called?

2. Put the following bridges in order of when they first opened: Brooklyn Bridge, Golden Gate Bridge, Eads Bridge.

3. What does the K in Kmart stand for?

4. What insect decimated the cotton crop in the American South in the early decades of the twentieth century?

5. What was the name of Benjamin Franklin's son who flew a kite into a thunderstorm in 1752?

6. What country was James Naismith, the inventor of basketball, from?

7. VY Canis Majoris is one of the largest stars ever discovered. What do astronomers classify such stars that can have a radius thousands of times greater than our own sun?

8. Within 10, how many elements are there on the periodic chart?

9. What is the hardest substance found in the human body?

10. What tribe was Sacagawea part of?

11. What UK female band released the hit *Cruel Summer* in 1983?

12. Unlike most horned animals, a rhinoceros horn is made entirely of what "K" fibrous protein?

13. Identify the name of the dog on *Married...with Children.*

14. Within five thousand miles (or 8 thousand km), what is the circumference of the Earth at the equator?

15. What were the New York Yankees called before they were the New York Yankees?

# Answer Sheet **Trivia Mix 4** **3 Rolls**	# Answer Sheet **Trivia Mix 4** **3 Rolls**	# Answer Sheet **Trivia Mix 4** **3 Rolls**
Name________________	**Name**________________	**Name**________________
1.	1.	1.
2.	2.	2.
3.	3.	3.
4.	4.	4.
5.	5.	5.
6.	6.	6.
7.	7.	7.
8.	8.	8.
9.	9.	9.
10.	10.	10.
11.	11.	11.
12.	12.	12.
13.	13.	13.
14.	14.	14.
15.	15.	15.

After you have filled out the sheet, fold your column underneath along the dashed line so the next restroom user won't see your answers. ***The first player uses the far right column.***

Notes:	***Notes:***	***Notes:***

Trivia Mix 5

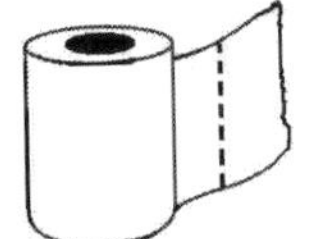

One Roll

1. On the Mott's logo, what is used for the apostrophe between the second T and the S?

2. What is "fax" an abbreviation for?

3. Who became Adolf Hitler's wife hours before he committed suicide?

4. What city is home to the Rock and Roll Hall of Fame?

5. How many sticks come in a small package of most brands of chewing gum?

6. What cooking product and household cleaning liquid consists mostly of acetic acid and water?

7. What red beverage mascot was known for busting through walls with a pitcher of refreshing drink?

8. What tops the Oxford English Corpus' list of the most frequently used words in the English language?

9. Who were the original three judges on *American Idol*?

10. Whose *Baby and Child Care* book has had 9 editions since it was first published in 1946?

11. Who did Roger Federer tie for a record 7th men's Wimbledon Title in 2012?

12. Of a fork, spoon, knife, or can-opener, which one has tines?

13. What number was Wayne Gretzky?

14. Who directed *The Godfather*?

15. In 1998, Fannie Mae Barnes became the first woman to operate what San Francisco mode of street transportation?

Answer Sheet Trivia Mix 5 1 Roll Name__________	**Answer Sheet** Trivia Mix 5 1 Roll Name__________	**Answer Sheet** Trivia Mix 5 1 Roll Name__________
1.	1.	1.
2.	2.	2.
3.	3.	3.
4.	4.	4.
5.	5.	5.
6.	6.	6.
7.	7.	7.
8.	8.	8.
9.	9.	9.
10.	10.	10.
11.	11.	11.
12.	12.	12.
13.	13.	13.
14.	14.	14.
15.	15.	15.

After you have filled out the sheet, fold your column underneath along the dashed line so the next restroom user won't see your answers. ***The first player uses the far right column.***

Notes:

Notes:

Notes:

Trivia Mix 5

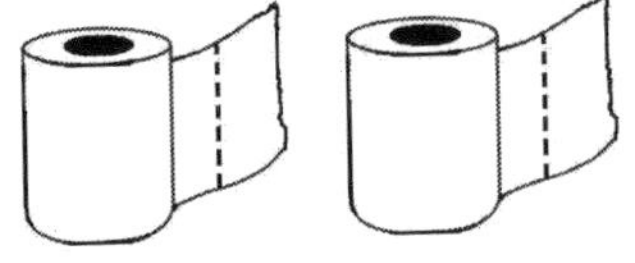

Two Rolls

1. Of Babe Ruth, Willie Mays, Lou Gehrig, and Ted Williams, who had the highest uniform number?

2. What 1994 breakthrough Green Day album featured the hits *Longview*, *She*, and *When I Come Around*?

3. What legendary comedic actor played a "Mog" (half man, half dog) named Barf in the Mel Brooks classic, *Spaceballs*?

4. In a World War II propaganda poster, what four word slogan was featured alongside an American woman flexing her muscle?

5. Along with Steve Ditko, what Marvel Comics legend created Spider-Man?

6. What is the name of the doctor running from the law in both the TV and movie versions of *The Fugitive*?

7. Who wrote the popular children's book *The Giving Tree*?

8. Of Justin Bieber, Lady Gaga, Katy Perry, and Barack Obama…who was the first to surpass 40 million Twitter followers?

9. What Spanish tomato and vegetable soup is usually served cold?

10. What does UPS stand for?

11. Within 3, how many peanut-segment-lines are on Mr. Peanut's body next to his cane?

12. What's pictured on the different Euro banknotes?

13. In what month of the year did the Titanic hit an iceberg?

14. Which river goes through the German cities of Cologne and Koblenz?

15. Who composed the *1812 Overture*?

Answer Sheet Trivia Mix 5 2 Rolls	Answer Sheet Trivia Mix 5 2 Rolls	Answer Sheet Trivia Mix 5 2 Rolls
Name____________	Name____________	Name____________
1.	1.	1.
2.	2.	2.
3.	3.	3.
4.	4.	4.
5.	5.	5.
6.	6.	6.
7.	7.	7.
8.	8.	8.
9.	9.	9.
10.	10.	10.
11.	11.	11.
12.	12.	12.
13.	13.	13.
14.	14.	14.
15.	15.	15.

After you have filled out the sheet, fold your column underneath along the dashed line so the next restroom user won't see your answers. ***The first player uses the far right column.***

Notes:	***Notes:***	***Notes:***

Trivia Mix 5

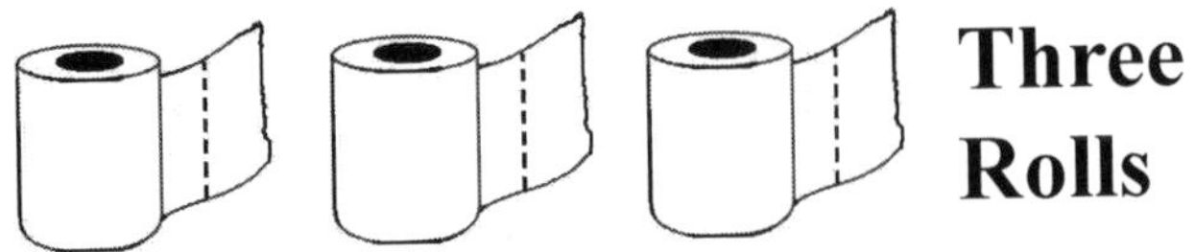

Three Rolls

1. Besides being friends, what financial relationship existed between the Mertzes and the Ricardos on *I Love Lucy*?

2. Within 5, how many quarters fit into a roll of US quarters?

3. What luxury-car logo features the letter “B” inside of a pair of wings?

4. Whose painting titled, *The Card Players*, sold for an unprecedented $259 million in 2011? It was purchased by the royal family of Qatar.

5. What was the name of Citizen Kane’s vast Floridian estate?

6. Which phylum are beetles in?

7. What type of “monsters” does TV personality Jeremy Wade try to catch?

8. What two provinces are home to the Canadian Rockies?

9. Who was the first President of NOW?

10. What does ESPN stand for?

11. Who co-founded Microsoft along with Bill Gates?

12. What’s the capital of Slovakia?

13. What small town in Pennsylvania is home to Phil, the Groundhog?

14. What does OPEC stand for?

15. What sport, played by ages 2-102, does the WMF regulate?

Answer Sheet

Trivia Mix 5
3 Rolls

Name____________________

1.
2.
3.
4.
5.
6.
7.
8.
9.
10.
11.
12.
13.
14.
15.

Answer Sheet

Trivia Mix 5
3 Rolls

Name____________________

1.
2.
3.
4.
5.
6.
7.
8.
9.
10.
11.
12.
13.
14.
15.

Answer Sheet

Trivia Mix 5
3 Rolls

Name____________________

1.
2.
3.
4.
5.
6.
7.
8.
9.
10.
11.
12.
13.
14.
15.

After you have filled out the sheet, fold your column underneath along the dashed line so the next restroom user won't see your answers. ***The first player uses the far right column.***

Notes:

Notes:

Notes:

Trivia Mix 6

Flip to pg. 83 for answers

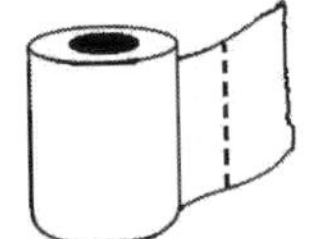

One Roll

1. Which Smurf seems to fix everything in the Smurf Village?

2. What NFL team's logo is the only one to have an eye-patch?

3. In November, 1863, politician Edward Everett was billed as the featured speaker at a government event and spoke for two hours. But what two-minute speech upstaged him?

4. Who murdered Lee Harvey Oswald on live TV?

5. In terms of New York museums, what does MoMA stand for?

6. What US state popularized gumbo?

7. In *Angry Birds*, what launches the birds through the air?

8. Which letter has the shortest code in Morse code?

9. What hunter did Bugs Bunny and Daffy Duck try to convince that it was duck or rabbit season?

10. What English monarch was known as "The Virgin Queen"?

11. What organization produces the most widely circulated magazine in the United States? You don't have to be over 50 to get this question right.

12. What color are the flowers that come out of a cucumber plant?

13. What McDonald's staple was first known as the Aristocrat, and the Blue Ribbon Burger?

14. What four letter "T" word do many use when referring to the London Underground?

15. Who played homicide detective, Columbo?

Answer Sheet Trivia Mix 6 1 Roll	**Answer Sheet** Trivia Mix 6 1 Roll	**Answer Sheet** Trivia Mix 6 1 Roll
Name____________	**Name**____________	**Name**____________
1.	1.	1.
2.	2.	2.
3.	3.	3.
4.	4.	4.
5.	5.	5.
6.	6.	6.
7.	7.	7.
8.	8.	8.
9.	9.	9.
10.	10.	10.
11.	11.	11.
12.	12.	12.
13.	13.	13.
14.	14.	14.
15.	15.	15.

After you have filled out the sheet, fold your column underneath along the dashed line so the next restroom user won't see your answers. ***The first player uses the far right column.***

Notes:	***Notes:***	***Notes:***

Trivia Mix 6

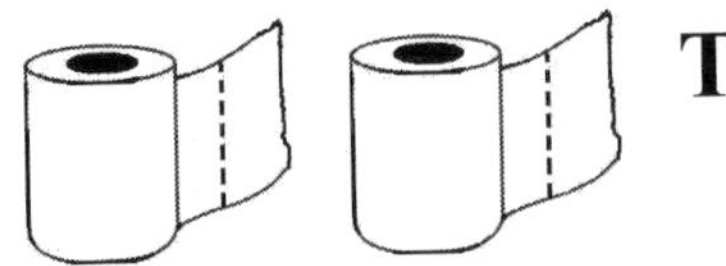

Two Rolls

1. On the color spectrum, what two colors is indigo between?

2. What is the wet nickname for the fifth and final community card flipped in a game of Texas Hold'em Poker?

3. What is the thickest layer of the Earth?

4. What "J" word refers to the fleshy part of an animal's cheek that droops down from the jaws?

5. If you poured a bowl of Lucky Charms in 1964, there would only be four different types of marshmallows in it. Name two of them.

6. Debuting in 1993, what New York City police drama pushed the envelope for nudity shown on television?

7. In 2000, Julia Roberts played a woman who looked to expose corporate pollution. What title-character and environmental activist did she play?

8. What colorful term is given to collegiate athletes looking to postpone their athletic eligibility for a year?

9. What bone is associated with the kneecap?

10. Of Conan O'Brien, Steve Allen, Jay Leno, and Joan Rivers, who was a guest host, but never the permanent host, of *The Tonight Show*?

11. What is the name of the symbol at the beginning of a musical staff which determines the pitch of notes?

12. Between radio and television, what Soap Opera was on the air for 72 years, from 1937-2009?

13. Who composed the famous operas *La Bohème* and *Madama Butterfly*?

14. Name one of the two South American countries that are not bordering Brazil.

15. As of 2013, what is the most circulated newspaper in the United States?

Answer Sheet **Trivia Mix 6** **2 Rolls**	**Answer Sheet** **Trivia Mix 6** **2 Rolls**	**Answer Sheet** **Trivia Mix 6** **2 Rolls**
Name________________	**Name**________________	**Name**________________
1.	1.	1.
2.	2.	2.
3.	3.	3.
4.	4.	4.
5.	5.	5.
6.	6.	6.
7.	7.	7.
8.	8.	8.
9.	9.	9.
10.	10.	10.
11.	11.	11.
12.	12.	12.
13.	13.	13.
14.	14.	14.
15.	15.	15.

After you have filled out the sheet, fold your column underneath along the dashed line so the next restroom user won't see your answers. ***The first player uses the far right column.***

Notes:	***Notes:***	***Notes:***

Trivia Mix 6

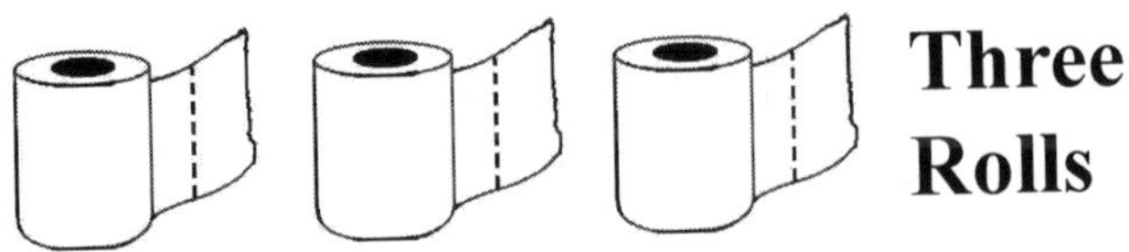

Three Rolls

1. What does *M*A*S*H* stand for?

2. What President is on the $1,000 bill?

3. What three colors make up the Belgium flag?

4. According to the United Nations Department of Economic and Social Affairs, what was the population of the Earth in the year 0? (Within 100 million)

5. What's the first name of the woman for whom the Taj Mahal was dedicated?

6. In 2013, who stepped in for CeeLo Green and Christina Aguilera and became coaches on Season 4 of *The Voice*?

7. What were "Okies"?

8. What is an eponym?

9. What two Houston Astros were known as the "Killer B's" from the 1990s through the early 2000s?

10. Which fish's roe does caviar traditionally come from?

11. What equation determines the circumference of a circle?

12. What was Groucho Marx's real first name?

13. What famed tight-rope walker did the unthinkable in 2013, when he crossed the Grand Canyon without a safety-net? He did it on live TV.

14. Who was the last US President to continuously sport a full beard?

15. Identify the Greek goddess of healing and cures.

Answer Sheet Trivia Mix 6 3 Rolls Name________	**Answer Sheet** Trivia Mix 6 3 Rolls Name________	**Answer Sheet** Trivia Mix 6 3 Rolls Name________
1.	1.	1.
2.	2.	2.
3.	3.	3.
4.	4.	4.
5.	5.	5.
6.	6.	6.
7.	7.	7.
8.	8.	8.
9.	9.	9.
10.	10.	10.
11.	11.	11.
12.	12.	12.
13.	13.	13.
14.	14.	14.
15.	15.	15.

After you have filled out the sheet, fold your column underneath along the dashed line so the next restroom user won't see your answers. ***The first player uses the far right column.***

Notes: ***Notes:*** ***Notes:***

Trivia Mix 7

Flip to pg. 86 for answers

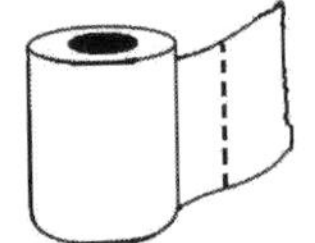

One Roll

1. Of veins and arteries, which carry blood *away* from the heart?

2. What phobia afflicts someone who is scared of spiders?

3. Professional wrestler Sylvester Ritter was better known as JYD. What was JYD short for?

4. What *Seinfeld* character wound up in a painting created by Jerry's then girlfriend? You can still buy it online.

5. What type of airplane do most commercial flights take place on?

6. What comedian was the original voice of Fat Albert?

7. What American city is home to the World of Coca-Cola?

8. What is the oldest Major League Baseball ballpark in the United States?

9. What "Title" of the Education Amendments of 1972 prevents gender discrimination in educational activities such as sports?

10. What two-word phrase refers to a group of people who suddenly start dancing, or doing something weird, for a short period of time in public?

11. Of a sleeve of golf balls, and a can of tennis balls, which one is pressurized?

12. In front of what memorial did Martin Luther King, Jr. deliver his *I Have a Dream* speech?

13. What company makes Tabasco Sauce?

14. What is the body of a boat called?

15. Of yellow, green, red, and purple, which color is not emitted from a firefly?

Answer Sheet **Trivia Mix 7** **1 Roll** **Name**____________	**Answer Sheet** **Trivia Mix 7** **1 Roll** **Name**____________	**Answer Sheet** **Trivia Mix 7** **1 Roll** **Name**____________
1.	1.	1.
2.	2.	2.
3.	3.	3.
4.	4.	4.
5.	5.	5.
6.	6.	6.
7.	7.	7.
8.	8.	8.
9.	9.	9.
10.	10.	10.
11.	11.	11.
12.	12.	12.
13.	13.	13.
14.	14.	14.
15.	15.	15.

After you have filled out the sheet, fold your column underneath along the dashed line so the next restroom user won't see your answers. ***The first player uses the far right column.***

Notes:	***Notes:***	***Notes:***

Trivia Mix 7

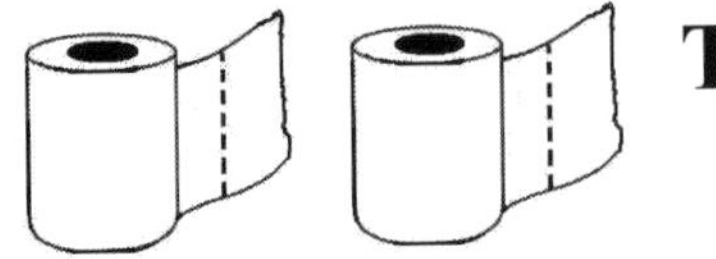

Two Rolls

1. From what part of a pig does ham come from?

2. In *Annie*, what is Oliver's last name?

3. What is the smallest box of Crayola Crayons to come with a built-in sharpener?

4. How did Charlie Harper, played by Charlie Sheen, die on *Two and a Half Men*?

5. In Dr. Seuss's *ABC: An Amazing Alphabet Book!*, which animal appears first?

6. You've heard it. You've seen it lip-synched. But who really sings *Call Me Maybe*?

7. What body system, which includes the pineal gland and hypothalamus, secretes various hormones?

8. Who was the first African American Supreme Court justice?

9. During the 1958-1960 model years, the Ford Motor Company produced a car called the Edsel. Where did they get the name Edsel?

10. The Black Sea cities of Yalta and Odessa used to be in the Soviet Union. What country are they in today?

11. What was the first capital of the US?

12. Within 4 mph either way, what are the minimum sustained winds required for a storm to be classified as a hurricane?

13. Who managed the Philadelphia Athletics for 50 years?

14. What state contains the only royal palace in the US?

15. Which Canadian folk singer immortalized the 1975 sinking of the SS *Edmund Fitzgerald*?

Answer Sheet

Trivia Mix 7
2 Rolls

Name____________________

1.
2.
3.
4.
5.
6.
7.
8.
9.
10.
11.
12.
13.
14.
15.

Answer Sheet

Trivia Mix 7
2 Rolls

Name____________________

1.
2.
3.
4.
5.
6.
7.
8.
9.
10.
11.
12.
13.
14.
15.

Answer Sheet

Trivia Mix 7
2 Rolls

Name____________________

1.
2.
3.
4.
5.
6.
7.
8.
9.
10.
11.
12.
13.
14.
15.

After you have filled out the sheet, fold your column underneath along the dashed line so the next restroom user won't see your answers. ***The first player uses the far right column.***

Notes:

Notes:

Notes:

Trivia Mix 7

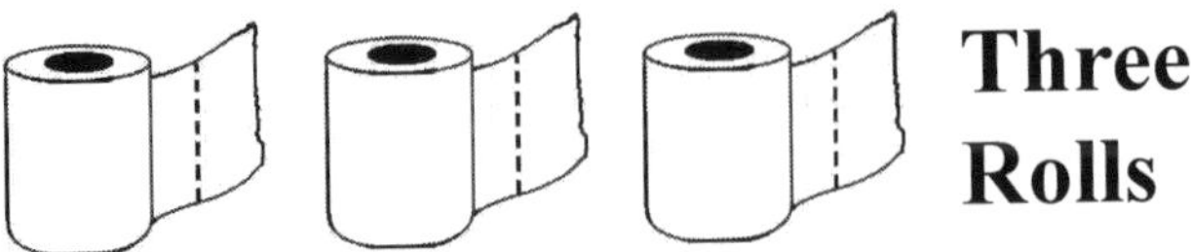

Flip to pg. 88 for answers

1. In commercial and photographic printing, what colors do the letters CMYK represent?

2. In 2011 and 2012, New York and New Jersey braced for two approaching hurricanes. Name them both.

3. How many inches in diameter were the original floppy disks?

4. What is a sommelier an expert in?

5. What celebrity won Season 1 of *Dancing with the Stars*?

6. Iran is one of the greatest producers of what nut?

7. What does a hygrometer measure?

8. What type of meat is in a traditional wiener schnitzel?

9. What do A.M. and P.M. stand for?

10. What is the longest river in Europe?

11. Name one of the two countries which claim to have invented the dance known as the tango?

12. What 1980s Boston Celtic, and later coach and basketball executive, was once an infielder for the Toronto Blue Jays?

13. What two very close Great Lakes are connected by the Straits of Mackinac?

14. What state is the geographical center of the contiguous United States?

15. Identify the Roman goddess of fate.

Answer Sheet Trivia Mix 7 3 Rolls Name______________	**Answer Sheet** Trivia Mix 7 3 Rolls Name______________	**Answer Sheet** Trivia Mix 7 3 Rolls Name______________
1.	1.	1.
2.	2.	2.
3.	3.	3.
4.	4.	4.
5.	5.	5.
6.	6.	6.
7.	7.	7.
8.	8.	8.
9.	9.	9.
10.	10.	10.
11.	11.	11.
12.	12.	12.
13.	13.	13.
14.	14.	14.
15.	15.	15.

After you have filled out the sheet, fold your column underneath along the dashed line so the next restroom user won't see your answers. ***The first player uses the far right column.***

Notes:

Notes:

Notes:

Trivia Mix 8

Flip to pg. 89 for answers

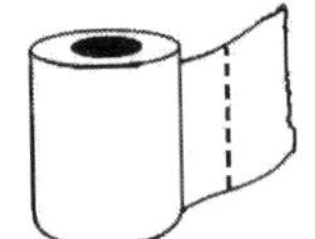

One Roll

1. Who was the host, and often writer, of *The Twilight Zone*?

2. How many strings are on the most common type of rock bass guitar?

3. What spud was the first toy to be advertised on television?

4. What is the capital of Spain?

5. On what sitcom do a few physics nerds find a beautiful woman living next door?

6. Which northern animal is the largest land carnivore on Earth?

7. What 2007 movie written by Seth Rogen and Evan Goldberg features a fake ID with the name "McLovin" on it?

8. What type of vegetable does the spice paprika come from?

9. Who hammered the 95 Theses, a statement protesting abuses of the Catholic Church, to a church door in Germany in 1517?

10. What city is home to the Parthenon?

11. What co-founder of Facebook was portrayed by Jesse Eisenberg in the 2010 film, *The Social Network*?

12. What action character from the novels of Robert Ludlum was later played by Matt Damon in a series of movies?

13. What pop-artist was known for expressing himself through Campbell's Soup cans?

14. What reality television show investigates the dangers of harvesting Alaskan crab in the Bering Sea?

15. What former basketball star led the NBA in rebounds for 7 consecutive seasons? In that time, he had more than 7 different hair colors as well.

Answer Sheet **Trivia Mix 8** **1 Roll**	**Answer Sheet** **Trivia Mix 8** **1 Roll**	**Answer Sheet** **Trivia Mix 8** **1 Roll**
Name____________	**Name**____________	**Name**____________
1.	1.	1.
2.	2.	2.
3.	3.	3.
4.	4.	4.
5.	5.	5.
6.	6.	6.
7.	7.	7.
8.	8.	8.
9.	9.	9.
10.	10.	10.
11.	11.	11.
12.	12.	12.
13.	13.	13.
14.	14.	14.
15.	15.	15.

After you have filled out the sheet, fold your column underneath along the dashed line so the next restroom user won't see your answers. ***The first player uses the far right column.***

Notes:	***Notes:***	***Notes:***

Trivia Mix 8

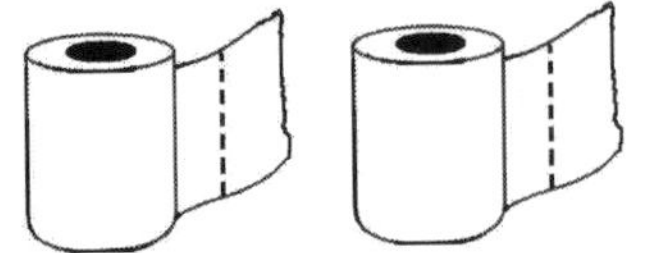

Two Rolls

1. In 1954, Syracuse Nationals (now the Philadelphia 76ers) owner Danny Biasone pushed for a new idea that would save the NBA from dying of boredom. What was it?

2. What word is given to the creamy paste of honey, sugar, and nuts that can be found in a candy bar?

3. How many oceans does Russia border?

4. Which Patriot kicked the game-winning field goal in Super Bowl XXXVIII? It was the same game where the halftime show involved the Janet Jackson *wardrobe malfunction.*

5. What mystery detective show starred Angela Lansbury as an author in a small Maine town?

6. What is the square root of 144?

7. What Serbian-American scientist, and rival of Thomas Edison, advanced today's alternating current (AC)?

8. Who do scientists believe to be the oldest ancestors of birds?

9. On *Scooby Doo*, what is the first name of the girl wearing glasses and an orange sweater?

10. Between automobiles, motorcycles, power equipment, and more, what company is the world's largest manufacturer of engines?

11. Alecia Beth Moore is better known as what "colorful" rock star? *So What* if you get this wrong.

12. At 49-0, which boxer was the only undefeated heavyweight champion of all time?

13. What company changed the office world with Spencer Silver's and Art Fry's invention of Post-it Notes?

14. What zodiac sign is associated with a crab?

15. Canadian wilderness expert Les Stroud is better known by what title?

Answer Sheet Trivia Mix 8 2 Rolls	**Answer Sheet** Trivia Mix 8 2 Rolls	**Answer Sheet** Trivia Mix 8 2 Rolls
Name____________	Name____________	Name____________
1.	1.	1.
2.	2.	2.
3.	3.	3.
4.	4.	4.
5.	5.	5.
6.	6.	6.
7.	7.	7.
8.	8.	8.
9.	9.	9.
10.	10.	10.
11.	11.	11.
12.	12.	12.
13.	13.	13.
14.	14.	14.
15.	15.	15.

After you have filled out the sheet, fold your column underneath along the dashed line so the next restroom user won't see your answers. ***The first player uses the far right column.***

Notes:	***Notes:***	***Notes:***

Trivia Mix 8

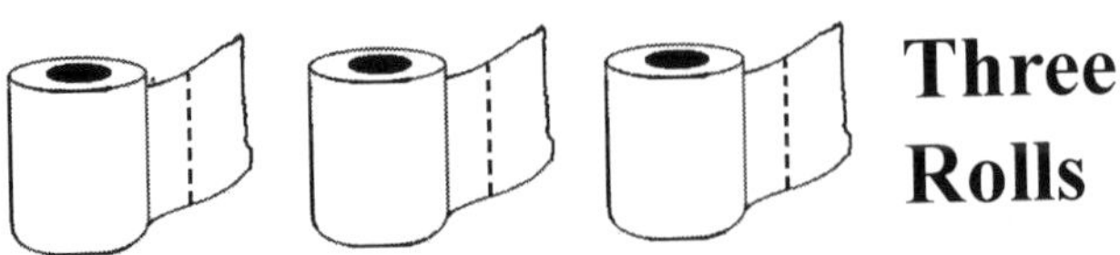

Flip to pg. 91 for answers

1. What does the ZIP in ZIP Code stand for?

2. Within 10, how many keys of an 88-key piano are black?

3. How many minutes of recording space are advertised on 4.7 GB blank DVDs?

4. Which of the following movies was longest in length? *JFK*, *The Hobbit: An Unexpected Journey*, or *The Godfather: Part II*?

5. Bisphenol A is a compound found in many plastics. What has been the more common abbreviation for Bisphenol A?

6. Within 50 years, what year was the Magna Carta signed?

7. What is the capital of Lebanon?

8. What is the name given to the following sequence of numbers: 1, 1, 2, 3, 5, 8, 13, 21, and 34?

9. Yellowstone's Old Faithful isn't really that faithful. It erupts irregularly. Within ten minutes, what does the National Park Service estimate to be the shortest time between eruptions?

10. Weezer's *Buddy Holly* music video "took place" at Arnold's Drive In Restaurant, on what 1970s and early 1980s sitcom?

11. Within two pounds, how much does a men's Olympic shot put weigh?

12. What composer's works included *The Barber of Seville* and *William Tell* (with its famous overture)?

13. What two actors were *Wedding Crashers* in 2005?

14. What Indian Empire developed the concept of zero and the decimal system?

15. What is the fifth largest continent in the world?

Answer Sheet	**Answer Sheet**	**Answer Sheet**
Trivia Mix 8 **3 Rolls**	**Trivia Mix 8** **3 Rolls**	**Trivia Mix 8** **3 Rolls**
Name________________	**Name**________________	**Name**________________
1.	1.	1.
2.	2.	2.
3.	3.	3.
4.	4.	4.
5.	5.	5.
6.	6.	6.
7.	7.	7.
8.	8.	8.
9.	9.	9.
10.	10.	10.
11.	11.	11.
12.	12.	12.
13.	13.	13.
14.	14.	14.
15.	15.	15.

After you have filled out the sheet, fold your column underneath along the dashed line so the next restroom user won't see your answers. ***The first player uses the far right column.***

Notes:	***Notes:***	***Notes:***

Trivia Mix 9

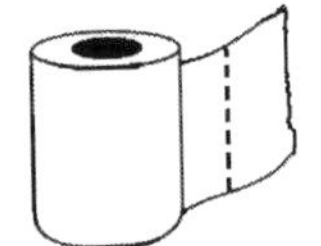

One Roll

1. In terms of surface area, what country holds the two largest lakes in Europe?

2. What did Prince William and Kate Middleton name their first child in 2013? (First name only)

3. In what 2012 hit song did R&B singer Janelle Monáe sing alongside the band Fun?

4. What vegetable has been known to cause a foul odor in urine?

5. What DC Super Friend has a lightning bolt on his chest?

6. According to a recent *New York Times* survey of local pizzerias, what topping is most frequently ordered?

7. Who narrates the science show *Through the Wormhole*? When in doubt, guess the usual narrator.

8. According to the old joke…how do you get to Carnegie Hall?

9. Who painted the *Mona Lisa*?

10. With five wins, what country's men's soccer team has won the most FIFA World Cups?

11. Why did Napoleon Bonaparte have a bad day on June 18, 1815?

12. In bowling, what numbered pin is in the far left corner?

13. What band's album, *Nevermind*, features a naked baby on the cover reaching for a dollar bill underwater?

14. Here's a toss-up. Are there more chickens in the world or humans?

15. How many justices sit on the US Supreme Court?

Answer Sheet **Trivia Mix 9** **1 Roll** **Name**________________	**Answer Sheet** **Trivia Mix 9** **1 Roll** **Name**________________	**Answer Sheet** **Trivia Mix 9** **1 Roll** **Name**________________
1.	1.	1.
2.	2.	2.
3.	3.	3.
4.	4.	4.
5.	5.	5.
6.	6.	6.
7.	7.	7.
8.	8.	8.
9.	9.	9.
10.	10.	10.
11.	11.	11.
12.	12.	12.
13.	13.	13.
14.	14.	14.
15.	15.	15.

After you have filled out the sheet, fold your column underneath along the dashed line so the next restroom user won't see your answers. ***The first player uses the far right column.***

Notes: | ***Notes:*** | ***Notes:***

Trivia Mix 9

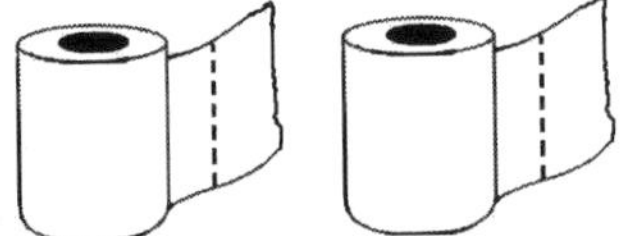

Two Rolls

1. What famous baseball field opened as Weeghman Park in 1914?

2. In terms of wireless technology, what does the G in 3G and 4G stand for?

3. What body organ produces insulin?

4. Besides Jim Morrison, name one other member of The Doors.

5. Co-creator of *King of the Hill*, Mike Judge was known earlier for creating what popular cartoon-duo seen on MTV?

6. What famous aviator is buried on the famous Road to Hana on the island of Maui?

7. What is the Yiddish word for cured salmon?

8. Which mountain has the highest peak in North America?

9. Squares, rectangles, parallelograms, and trapezoids are all classified as what type of polygon?

10. Name 4 of the “Original Six” NHL Hockey teams.

11. One of the most printed works of the twentieth century, what did the Chinese government encourage people to carry with them during the 1960s and 1970s?

12. What English entertainer and journalist famously interviewed former President Richard Nixon in 1977? The interviews became the subject of a 2008 movie.

13. What is the longest bone in the body?

14. What is the closest spiral galaxy to our own?

15. Before 1500, what world empire took over more land than any other in human history?

Answer Sheet Trivia Mix 9 2 Rolls	**Answer Sheet** Trivia Mix 9 2 Rolls	**Answer Sheet** Trivia Mix 9 2 Rolls
Name____________	**Name**____________	**Name**____________
1.	1.	1.
2.	2.	2.
3.	3.	3.
4.	4.	4.
5.	5.	5.
6.	6.	6.
7.	7.	7.
8.	8.	8.
9.	9.	9.
10.	10.	10.
11.	11.	11.
12.	12.	12.
13.	13.	13.
14.	14.	14.
15.	15.	15.

After you have filled out the sheet, fold your column underneath along the dashed line so the next restroom user won't see your answers. ***The first player uses the far right column.***

Notes:	***Notes:***	***Notes:***

Trivia Mix 9

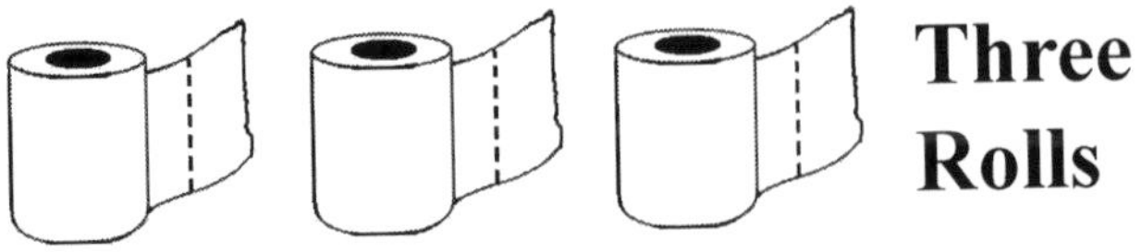

Flip to pg. 94 for answers

1. Who was born Robert Allen Zimmerman on May 24, 1941?

2. What 7 minute time periods make up a polo match?

3. Give one of the first names of either Dow or Jones.

4. What extinct sea predator grew to over 60 feet long, and with its 7 inch-long teeth, could have taken off a whale's tail with one bite?

5. Which country regulates the Galapagos Islands?

6. Name two of the three bright stars that make up the Winter Triangle. One is found in Orion.

7. What 20th century American singer was known as "The Velvet Fog"?

8. What was the most popular baby girl name in the United States for 2012? Starts with S.

9. What is the yellow discharge *cerumen* better known as?

10. The now-extinct Talbot and Southern hounds are related to what common household friend?

11. What was the first Beach Boys single to reach Number 1 in the United States?

12. How many ounces are in a cup?

13. What long "A" word means the period before the Great Flood?

14. What model of car does canine Brian Griffin drive on *Family Guy*?

15. What was the name of the group that provided vocal background for Elvis Presley from 1956-1970?

Answer Sheet Trivia Mix 9 3 Rolls Name______________	Answer Sheet Trivia Mix 9 3 Rolls Name______________	Answer Sheet Trivia Mix 9 3 Rolls Name______________
1.	1.	1.
2.	2.	2.
3.	3.	3.
4.	4.	4.
5.	5.	5.
6.	6.	6.
7.	7.	7.
8.	8.	8.
9.	9.	9.
10.	10.	10.
11.	11.	11.
12.	12.	12.
13.	13.	13.
14.	14.	14.
15.	15.	15.

After you have filled out the sheet, fold your column underneath along the dashed line so the next restroom user won't see your answers. ***The first player uses the far right column.***

Notes:

Notes:

Notes:

Trivia Mix 10

Flip to pg. 95 for answers

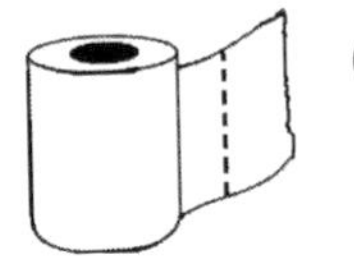

One Roll

1. On most software programs, what key stroke will get you to Help?

2. What's the name of Thomas Jefferson's home in Charlottesville, Virginia?

3. In our solar system, which is the largest planet?

4. What two-letter nickname do most people use when referring to multiple-sport athlete Vincent Jackson?

5. What boy was tricked into burying his gold coins at the Field of Miracles?

6. How many rings are on the Olympic flag?

7. In the song *Wheels on the Bus*, what do the wipers go?

8. Which category of long-life batteries comes in AA, AAA, C, D, and 9V?

9. What type of mustard was created by Jean Naigeon when he replaced vinegar with the juice from unripe grapes?

10. What is the name of the vehicle that resurfaces the ice between hockey periods?

11. What tire and rubber company's fleet of blimps have been spotted in skies since 1925?

12. What color is the girl's hat on a box of Sun-Maid Raisins?

13. Who led the orchestra on most nights of *The Tonight Show Starring Johnny Carson*?

14. What term refers to two words which sound the same, but have different meanings?

15. Which US state is "The Peach State"?

Answer Sheet Trivia Mix 10 1 Roll	Answer Sheet Trivia Mix 10 1 Roll	Answer Sheet Trivia Mix 10 1 Roll
Name__________	Name__________	Name__________
1.	1.	1.
2.	2.	2.
3.	3.	3.
4.	4.	4.
5.	5.	5.
6.	6.	6.
7.	7.	7.
8.	8.	8.
9.	9.	9.
10.	10.	10.
11.	11.	11.
12.	12.	12.
13.	13.	13.
14.	14.	14.
15.	15.	15.

After you have filled out the sheet, fold your column underneath along the dashed line so the next restroom user won't see your answers. ***The first player uses the far right column.***

Notes:	***Notes:***	***Notes:***

Trivia Mix 10

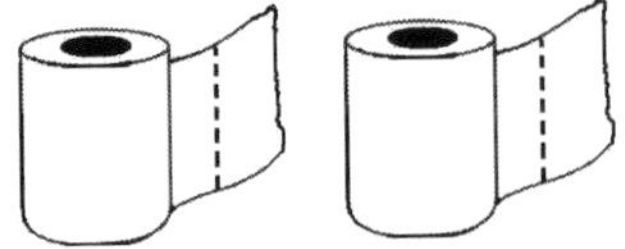

Two Rolls

1. How many people were stranded on *Gilligan's Island*?

2. What is the only New York City borough attached to the New York mainland?

3. What muscle makes up the largest part of the human buttocks?

4. With a consistency similar to rotini, what is the name given to long corkscrew shaped pasta?

5. Who are the only two US Presidents to be impeached?

6. What two actors depicted Willy Wonka on the big screen in 1971 and 2005?

7. What waterway did Hernando De Soto explore in 1541, and die near in 1542?

8. What does a barometer measure?

9. Rachael Ray helped popularize the term "EVOO" in kitchens across America. What does it stand for?

10. The 1961 movie, *The Misfits*, was the last full-feature film for two Hollywood icons that passed away shortly thereafter. Clark Gable was one. Who was the other?

11. What band formed after auditioning individually for *The X-Factor* in 2010?

12. Who wrote *Of Mice and Men*?

13. If you were texting, and wanted to add some cool glasses to your smiley face, what number or letter would you use?

14. What TV reality show, hosted by Anderson Cooper, featured a person who was deliberately trying to prevent the other contestants from making money?

15. Before Ringo Starr, who was the drummer for the Beatles?

Answer Sheet

Trivia Mix 10
2 Rolls

Name__________________

1.
2.
3.
4.
5.
6.
7.
8.
9.
10.
11.
12.
13.
14.
15.

Answer Sheet

Trivia Mix 10
2 Rolls

Name__________________

1.
2.
3.
4.
5.
6.
7.
8.
9.
10.
11.
12.
13.
14.
15.

Answer Sheet

Trivia Mix 10
2 Rolls

Name__________________

1.
2.
3.
4.
5.
6.
7.
8.
9.
10.
11.
12.
13.
14.
15.

After you have filled out the sheet, fold your column underneath along the dashed line so the next restroom user won't see your answers. ***The first player uses the far right column.***

Notes:

Notes:

Notes:

Trivia Mix 10

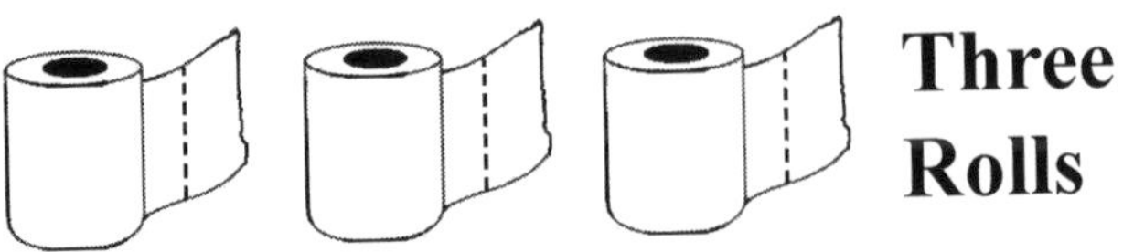

Three Rolls

1. Name the singer of "historical" songs such as *Sink the Bismarck*, *Battle of New Orleans*, and *North to Alaska*. He died in an auto accident on November 5, 1960.

2. What colorful creature's skin was historically used to make poisonous darts in South America?

3. What popular children's book starts with an owl and ends with a mirror?

4. Designed in the mid-1980s, what toy ball has long rubber fibers protruding from its center? Those strings sure make it easier to catch.

5. What state is home to Bryce Canyon?

6. What title is given to the "first bishop" and leader of the Church of England?

7. Besides Spain and Portugal, what tiny sovereign nation's borders rest on the Iberian Peninsula?

8. It would be almost five decades before anyone came close to this golfer's record of all-time PGA Tour wins. Name him.

9. How many flat sides are there on a dodecahedron?

10. This Italian ocean liner collided with the MS *Stockholm* and sank off the coast of Nantucket in 1956.

11. With regards to a volcano, what's lahar?

12. What famous 1925 trial involved a teacher's controversial teaching of the theory of evolution in a Tennessee classroom?

13. What is the largest organ of the human body?

14. Who was the runner-up to Kelly Clarkson in Season 1 of *American Idol*?

15. What do the words education, abstemious, and facetious all have in common?

Answer Sheet

Trivia Mix 10
3 Rolls

Name________________

Answer Sheet

Trivia Mix 10
3 Rolls

Name________________

Answer Sheet

Trivia Mix 10
3 Rolls

Name________________

1.	1.	1.
2.	2.	2.
3.	3.	3.
4.	4.	4.
5.	5.	5.
6.	6.	6.
7.	7.	7.
8.	8.	8.
9.	9.	9.
10.	10.	10.
11.	11.	11.
12.	12.	12.
13.	13.	13.
14.	14.	14.
15.	15.	15.

After you have filled out the sheet, fold your column underneath along the dashed line so the next restroom user won't see your answers. ***The first player uses the far right column.***

Notes:

Notes:

Notes:

Trivia Mix 1

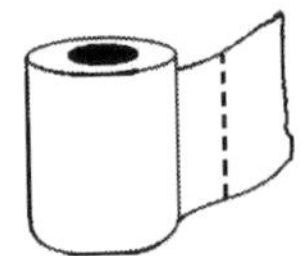

One Roll — Answers

1. Red
2. William H. Taft was over 300 pounds, and once got stuck in the White House bathtub
3. A1 Steak Sauce
4. Madagascar
5. Richard Pryor. It was recorded in 1971, but released in 1985. The fire was in 1980.
6. Oregano
7. Published in 2003, Dan Brown's *The Da Vinci Code* has sold over 80 million copies as of 2013
8. Thirteen
9. Pacific Ocean
10. 29
11. *The Italian Stallion*
12. Butter/margarine and milk
13. Scranton
14. Woodstock
15. Milky Way

Trivia Mix 1

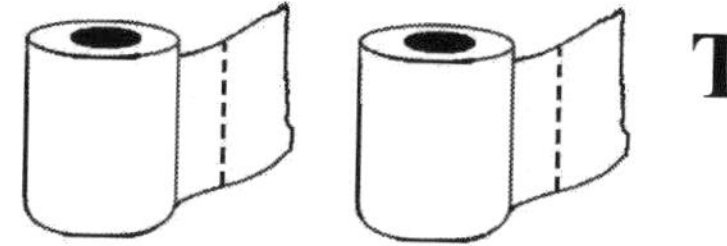

Two Rolls — Answers

1. A quarter, or 25 cents
2. Six. Chandler, Joey, Monica, Phoebe, Rachel, Ross
3. Lima beans. Lima is the capital of Peru.
4. Play-Doh
5. Giant squid
6. The Spanish brought horses over to the New World during colonization
7. Beyoncé, who won the same amount in 2010
8. Halley's Comet. Twain was 74 when he died.
9. As of 2013, the Yankees have won 27 World Series. The Canadiens have won 24 Stanley Cups. Michael Phelps has won 22 Olympic medals.
10. Roanoke
11. Jor-El
12. Langston Hughes. The title can be found within the poem *Harlem* (also called *A Dream Deferred*).
13. Cicadas. We will accept locusts.
14. Reserve Officers' Training Corps
15. Yellow, with green lettering

Trivia Mix 1

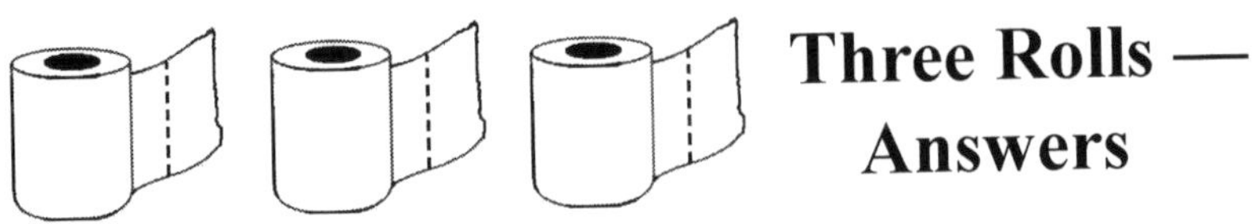

Three Rolls — Answers

1. Rheum
2. E.L. James, the pseudonym of Erika Leonard
3. Hindi (Hindustani)
4. Bull and Finch Pub
5. David “Deacon” Jones
6. Archie, short for Archive, was programmed by Alan Emtage
7. Scantron
8. *Richard II*
9. Arizona, on Valentine’s Day
10. Words such as *racecar*, or phrases such as, *As I pee Sir, I see Pisa* are called palindromes
11. Isobars
12. *Puck Man*
13. Grape Ape, of *The Great Grape Ape Show*
14. Mariana Trench in the Pacific Ocean. It’s 35,840 feet deep.
15. Miami Heat, Oklahoma City Thunder, Orlando Magic, Utah Jazz

Trivia Mix 2

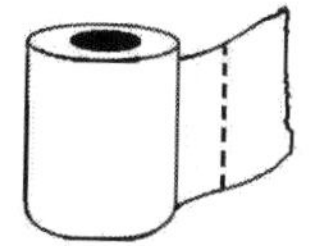

One Roll — Answers

1. Male. XX is female.
2. *The Fresh Prince of Bel-Air*
3. Black and Orange. He also traditionally wears a turquoise tie.
4. Driver
5. *Raiders of the Lost Ark*
6. Napa
7. Adverbs
8. Gherkins
9. Special Victims Unit
10. Best Buy
11. The sun
12. Diego, of *Go, Diego, Go!*
13. John Wilkes Booth
14. Running of the Bulls
15. T-shirt (tee shirt)

Trivia Mix 2

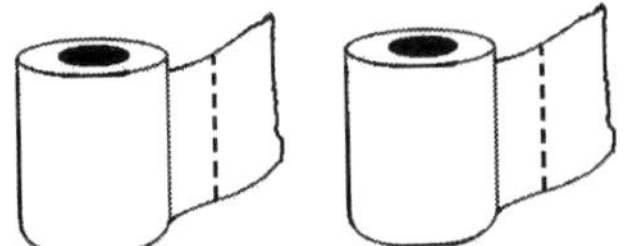

Two Rolls — Answers

1. Yiddish

2. Garry Shandling

3. *The Avengers* grossed about $1.5 billion in 2012

4. Two weeks

5. South America, in the Andes Mountains

6. Greyhound. In recent years, greyhounds have become the focus of a rescue and adoption movement to help those no longer used in the racing industry.

7. Robin Quivers

8. Silver

9. Twenty-four notes

10. The Swiss Guards

11. China has about a dozen cities which not only begin with X, but have close to, or over, one million people living there. Xi'an was the ancient capital.

12. Seven

13. Milk chocolate, California raisins, and roasted peanuts

14. Cooperstown, home of the National Baseball Hall of Fame

15. They are outgoing, talkative, and sociable

Trivia Mix 2

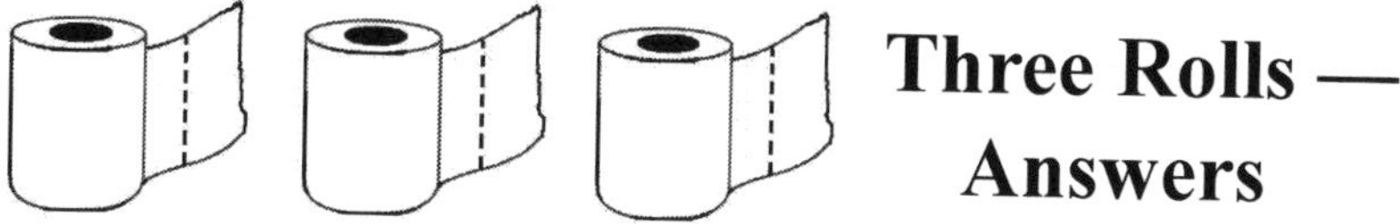

Three Rolls — Answers

1. 23 flavors

2. Newfoundland and Labrador

3. Ernesto Miranda. Not knowing he had a right to remain silent, Miranda confessed to several felonies. The Supreme Court took his side in 1966, and he had to be retried. He was in and out of prison for years, and later died in a bar fight in 1976. He was known to autograph Miranda warning cards.

4. Crosley Field in Cincinnati. The Reds beat the Phillies 2-1 in front of 20,422 fans on May 24, 1935.

5. Gavrilo Princip, a Serbian nationalist

6. File Transfer Protocol

7. 29½ days

8. A tittle

9. Link

10. Avocado

11. Pheidippides. He ran from the Battle of Marathon to Athens, and died after delivering his news.

12. Quaker Oats. It was registered as a man in Quaker clothing.

13. Bruce Springsteen's *Born in the U.S.A.* was the first to be manufactured in the USA

14. Participle

15. Hippodrome. The name is sometimes used today for theatrical venues.

Trivia Mix 3

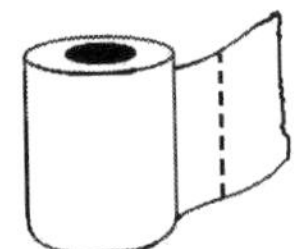

One Roll — Answers

1. Slinky
2. Wonder Woman
3. Dolley Madison
4. Pantalones
5. George Burns in 1996, and Bob Hope in 2003
6. Romaine lettuce
7. Tsunami
8. A duck. The voice was done by Gilbert Gottfried. He was later replaced.
9. Yosemite National Park
10. NaCl, or sodium chloride
11. Lock
12. The Bible has sold billions of copies
13. Five
14. Truck
15. Bic. The Bic Cristal quickly spread around the world.

Trivia Mix 3

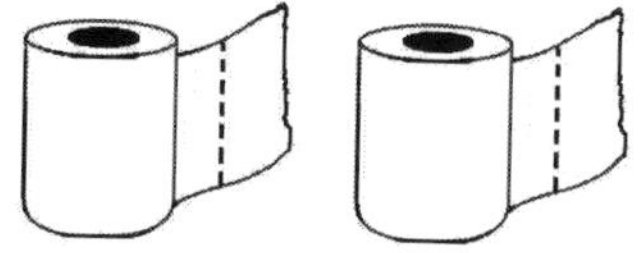

Two Rolls — Answers

1. Charlotte Brontë
2. Iran
3. Eight
4. Golda Meir
5. Linda Ronstadt
6. *Frère Jacques*
7. Underoos
8. Nebula
9. Fifty-five
10. Tobacco
11. Dry Ice
12. *Live Free or Die*
13. Peter the Great
14. Three, if you are the owl from the commercial. But, "the world may never know."
15. Hawaii

Trivia Mix 3

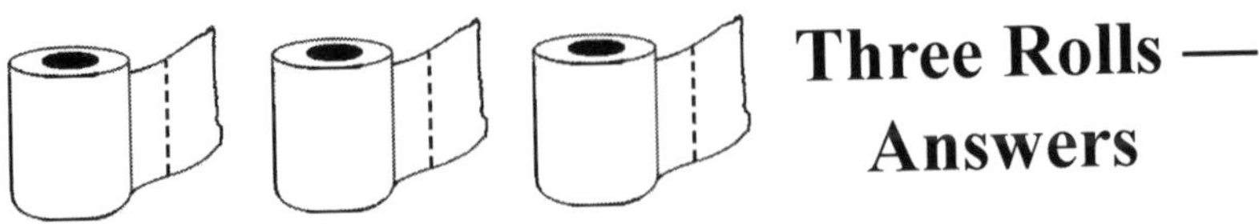

Three Rolls — Answers

1. Pleistocene

2. Eight

3. Granny Smith apples

4. Fifty-six

5. Snakes

6. Deoxyribonucleic acid

7. Carl Yastrzemski of the Boston Red Sox also led the league in batting average, home runs, and runs batted in

8. Bangladesh

9. The shilling

10. Vanilla, Chocolate, Mint Chocolate Chip, Pralines 'n Cream, and Chocolate Chip

11. Cherilyn Sarkisian

12. Barlow lens

13. The 1983 NFL Draft. Six quarterbacks were taken in the first round, setting a new draft record.

14. Jacob

15. *Don Quixote* has been estimated to have sold over 500 million copies

Trivia Mix 4

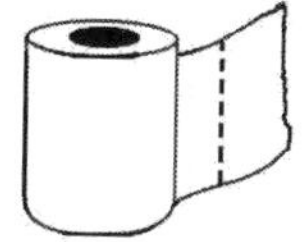

One Roll — Answers

1. Morgan Freeman
2. Andrew Jackson
3. Afghanistan
4. King Kandy
5. Seven and nine. Unlike on older phones, Q has now been added to seven, and Z was put on top of nine.
6. Whitney Houston
7. Clint Eastwood
8. Machu Picchu
9. African ones have larger ears. African elephants are also unique in that both sexes will always have visible tusks.
10. Pasta. It's in the shape of rice.
11. Dippin' Dots
12. *Scrabble*
13. Casing
14. *Survivor*
15. The Rock

Trivia Mix 4

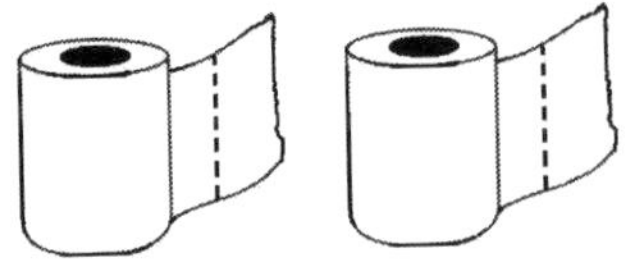

Two Rolls — Answers

1. None of the inductees were alive to revel in the glory

2. 32 teeth

3. Three strikes in a row

4. Willie Sutton. He pitched ID cards for Connecticut's New Britain Bank & Trust Co.

5. St. Augustine. The city was founded by the Spanish in 1565.

6. Waikiki Beach

7. Electronic Arts, Inc.

8. Thomas Jefferson. The Department of Agriculture estimates that the average person consumes about 50 pounds of frozen potatoes per year… most of which are similar to Jefferson's serving suggestion.

9. Istanbul

10. As of 2013, *Harry Potter* has 8 films. *Star Wars* has 6, and *The Lord of the Rings* has 3.

11. Numerator (top) and denominator (bottom)

12. Danny DeVito

13. Bill Russell of the Boston Celtics won 11 times. Henri Richard of the Montreal Canadiens won 11 Stanley Cups. He and Russell are tied for the most titles won in North American professional sports.

14. The number 4

15. The Red Baron

Trivia Mix 4

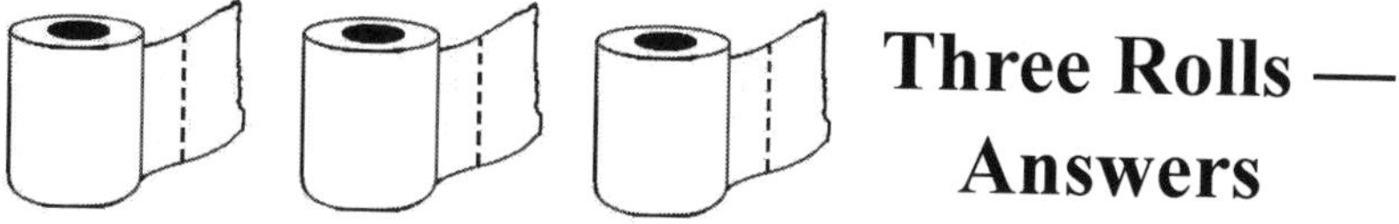

Three Rolls — Answers

1. Rods and cones

2. Eads Bridge (1874), Brooklyn Bridge (1883), Golden Gate Bridge (1937). To calm fears of the Eads Bridge collapsing over the Mississippi, an elephant was sent over as a test before it opened. The elephant made it safely to the other side.

3. Kresge. It was founded by Sebastian Spering Kresge

4. Boll weevil

5. William. Myth says he was a kid, but he was in his early 20s at the time.

6. Canada

7. Hypergiants

8. 118…that is until something new is discovered

9. Tooth enamel. It's also the most mineralized entity as well.

10. Shoshone

11. Bananarama

12. Keratin

13. Buck

14. 24,901.55 miles (40,075.16 kilometers)

15. They were the New York Highlanders until 1912. They played in Hilltop Park, one of the highest points in New York City.

Trivia Mix 5

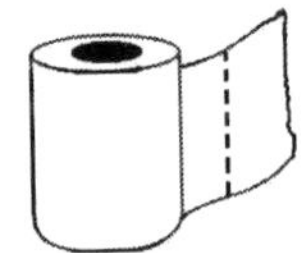

One Roll — Answers

1. A leaf, or apple stem
2. Facsimile
3. Eva Braun
4. Cleveland, Ohio
5. Five sticks of gum
6. Vinegar
7. Kool-Aid Man
8. The
9. Randy Jackson, Paula Abdul, and Simon Cowell
10. Dr. Benjamin Spock
11. Pete Sampras
12. Fork. Tines are the prongs of the fork.
13. 99
14. Francis Ford Coppola
15. Cable Car

Trivia Mix 5

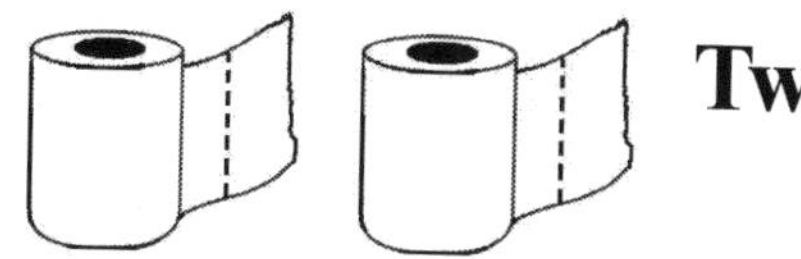

Two Rolls — Answers

1. Mays wore number 24. Ruth was 3, Gehrig was 4, and Williams was 9.
2. *Dookie*
3. John Candy
4. We Can Do It!
5. Stan Lee
6. Dr. Richard Kimble
7. Shel Silverstein
8. Justin Bieber eclipsed the total in 2013
9. Gazpacho
10. United Parcel Service
11. Six
12. Architectural styles reflecting cultural periods
13. April. It sank on April 15, 1912.
14. Rhine River
15. Pyotr Tchaikovsky

Trivia Mix 5

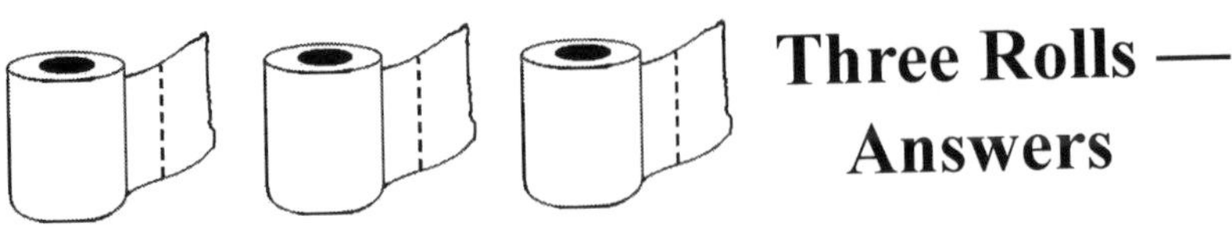

Three Rolls — Answers

1. Fred and Ethel Mertz were Ricky and Lucy Ricardo's landlords

2. Forty, or $10 worth

3. Bentley

4. Paul Cézanne

5. Xanadu

6. Arthropoda, or Arthropods

7. Fish. The angler is famous for catching rare and large species of *River Monsters*.

8. Alberta and British Columbia

9. Betty Friedan was also a founder of the National Organization for Women

10. Entertainment and Sports Programming Network

11. Paul Allen

12. Bratislava

13. Punxsutawney is home for Phil, the famous groundhog of Groundhog Day (February 2). If he sees his shadow, it means six more weeks of bad weather, and he returns to his hole. If he doesn't see it, it means spring is near, and he stays outside. It's an inexact science.

14. Organization of the Petroleum Exporting Countries

15. Miniature golf. It's the World Minigolf Sport Federation. Yes, there are rules.

Trivia Mix 6

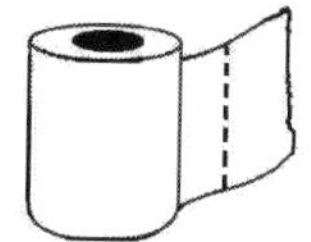

One Roll — Answers

1. Handy Smurf
2. Oakland Raiders
3. Abraham Lincoln's Gettysburg Address
4. Jack Ruby, two days after Oswald assassinated John F. Kennedy
5. Museum of Modern Art
6. Louisiana
7. A slingshot
8. E…it was made the shortest because it's the letter used most often. It is one dot.
9. Elmer Fudd
10. Elizabeth I
11. AARP (American Association of Retired Persons)
12. Yellow
13. Big Mac
14. Tube
15. Peter Falk

Trivia Mix 6

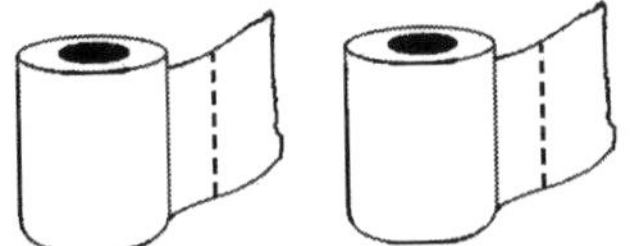

Two Rolls — Answers

1. Blue and Violet (ROYGBIV)
2. River card
3. Mantle. It's about 1,800 miles thick.
4. Jowl
5. Hearts, Stars, Clovers, and Moons were the original four marshmallows
6. *NYPD Blue*
7. Erin Brockovich
8. Redshirt
9. Patella
10. Joan Rivers guest hosted 93 times for Johnny Carson
11. Clef
12. *Guiding Light/The Guiding Light*. It is credited as being the longest running daytime drama of all time.
13. Giacomo Puccini
14. Chile and Ecuador
15. *The Wall Street Journal*

Trivia Mix 6

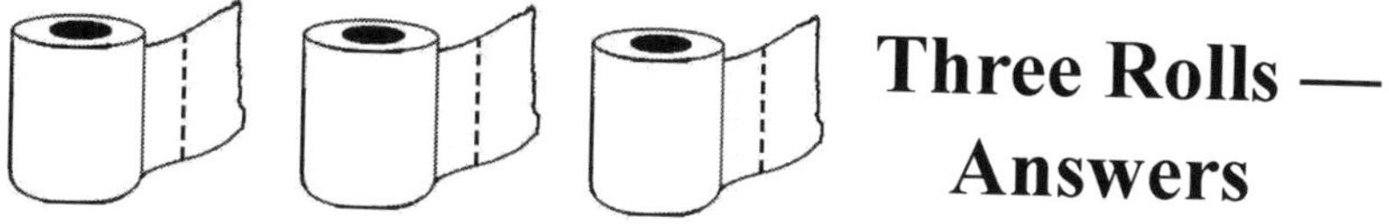

Three Rolls — Answers

1. Mobile Army Surgical Hospital
2. Grover Cleveland
3. Black, yellow, and red
4. 300 million people
5. Mumtaz. Mumtaz Mahal was the wife of Shah Jahan. She was also known as Arjumand Banu Begum. After she died, the structure was erected in her honor.
6. Usher and Shakira
7. People who migrated to California during the Dust Bowl of the 1930s. Many came from Oklahoma.
8. A person after whom an idea, discovery, invention, or place is named. For example, Washington DC was named for George Washington.
9. Craig Biggio and Jeff Bagwell
10. Sturgeon
11. $2\pi r$
12. Julius
13. Nick Wallenda
14. Benjamin Harrison
15. Panacea

Trivia Mix 7

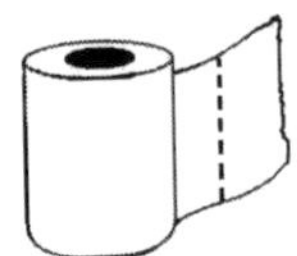

One Roll — Answers

1. Arteries. Remember A for Away.
2. Arachnophobia
3. Junkyard Dog
4. Kramer was portrayed in *The Kramer*
5. Boeing 747
6. Bill Cosby
7. Atlanta, Georgia
8. Fenway Park in Boston, Massachusetts
9. Title IX
10. Flash mob
11. Both come in groups of three, but tennis balls are pressurized in the can
12. Lincoln Memorial
13. McIlhenny Company
14. Hull
15. Purple

Trivia Mix 7

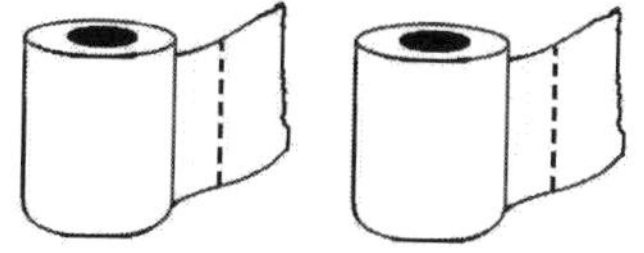

Two Rolls — Answers

1. Hind legs, or thigh
2. Warbucks. Daddy Warbucks has a first name, and it's Oliver.
3. Sixty-four crayons. It also comes on larger boxes.
4. He was hit by a subway train
5. Alligator
6. Carly Rae Jepsen
7. Endocrine system
8. Thurgood Marshall was appointed by President Lyndon Johnson in 1967
9. Edsel Ford was the son of Henry Ford
10. Ukraine
11. New York. George Washington was inaugurated on the balcony of Federal Hall on April 30, 1789.
12. 74 mph
13. Connie Mack
14. Iolani Palace is in Honolulu, Hawaii. It was built in 1882 for King Kalakaua.
15. Gordon Lightfoot

Trivia Mix 7

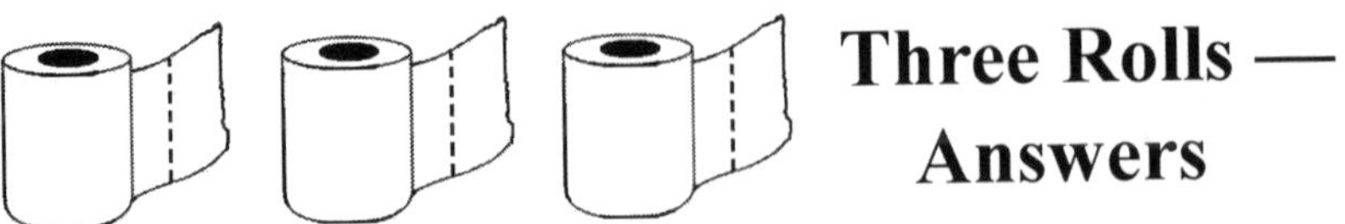

Three Rolls — Answers

1. Cyan, Magenta, Yellow, and Key. But "key" is really black, because it comes from the black "key plate" used in printing.

2. Irene in 2011, and Sandy in 2012

3. Eight inches. They were introduced by IBM in 1971, and gradually went downward in size to 5¼ and 3½ inches in diameter.

4. Wine

5. Kelly Monaco of *General Hospital* won with professional dancer Alec Mazo

6. Pistachio

7. Humidity

8. Veal

9. It's Latin for ante meridiem and post meridiem, referring to before and after midday

10. The Volga is 2,294 miles long. The Danube is second at 1,777 miles long.

11. Argentina and Uruguay

12. Danny Ainge

13. Lake Michigan and Lake Huron

14. Kansas. There is a marker near Lebanon, KS that indicates the location.

15. Fortuna

Trivia Mix 8

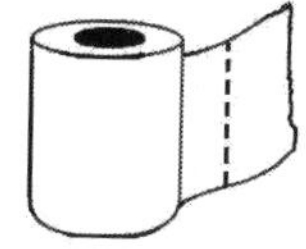

One Roll — Answers

1. Rod Serling
2. Four strings
3. Mr. Potato Head, in 1952
4. Madrid
5. *The Big Bang Theory*
6. Bear. Both Kodiak and polar bears are considered the biggest.
7. *Superbad*
8. Peppers
9. Martin Luther
10. Athens, Greece
11. Mark Zuckerberg
12. Jason Bourne
13. Andy Warhol
14. *Deadliest Catch*
15. Dennis Rodman

Trivia Mix 8

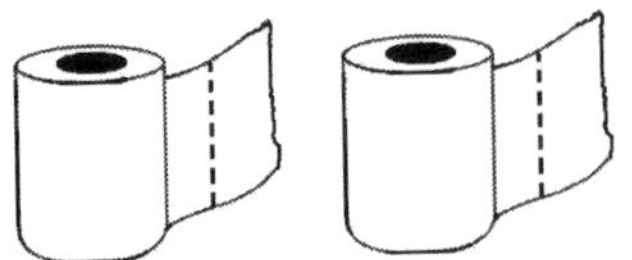

Two Rolls — Answers

1. The 24-second shot clock
2. Nougat
3. Three: Atlantic (through the Baltic and Black Seas), Pacific, and Arctic
4. Adam Vinatieri booted a 41-yard field goal with four seconds to go to give the New England Patriots a 32-29 win over the Carolina Panthers.
5. *Murder, She Wrote*
6. Twelve
7. Nikola Tesla. Edison used AC to fuel the electric chair. He was hoping to show the dangers of Tesla's current. However, most current used to power homes today is AC.
8. Dinosaurs
9. Velma
10. Honda
11. P!nk, or Pink
12. Rocky Marciano. 43 of his 49 wins were by knockout.
13. 3M
14. Cancer
15. *Survivorman*

Trivia Mix 8

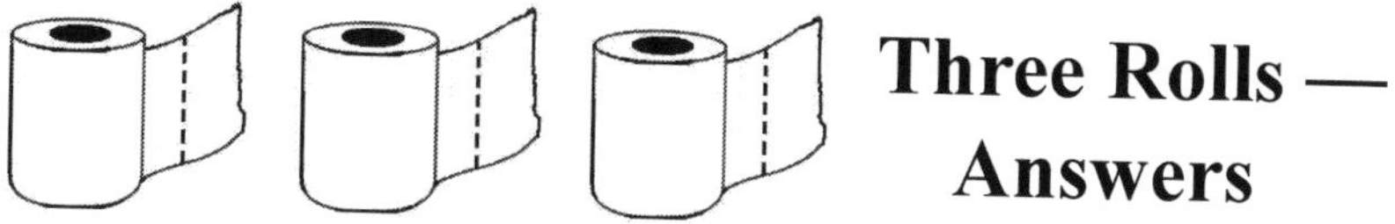

Three Rolls — Answers

1. Zone Improvement Plan, which began in 1963

2. Thirty-six. There are fifty-two white ones.

3. 120 minutes

4. *The Godfather: Part II* was 200 minutes long. *JFK* ran for 189 minutes. *The Hobbit: An Unexpected Journey* was 169 minutes in length.

5. BPA, as in BPA-free

6. 1215

7. Beirut

8. Fibonacci numbers, where each number is the sum of the previous two. This sequence appears in certain natural phenomenon, such as the curves of waves and patterns of shells.

9. One hour. They estimate the time to be between 60-110 minutes. Of course, there are always anomalies.

10. *Happy Days*. It was obviously done through special effects, as the sitcom went off the air a decade earlier.

11. Sixteen pounds

12. Gioachino Rossini

13. Vince Vaughn and Owen Wilson

14. Gupta Empire

15. Antarctica. Antarctica is bigger than Europe, and just less than twice the size of Australia.

Trivia Mix 9

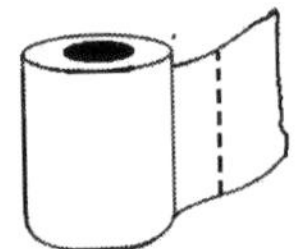

One Roll — Answers

1. Russia. In size order, it's Lake Ladoga and Lake Onega. Russia also contains the largest lake by volume in the world, Lake Baikal, but it's in Asia.

2. George. The full name is George Alexander Louis of Cambridge.

3. *We are Young*

4. Asparagus. Doctors say it's more potent in some people than in others.

5. The Flash

6. Pepperoni

7. Morgan Freeman

8. Practice, practice, practice

9. Leonardo da Vinci

10. Brazil

11. He was defeated at the Battle of Waterloo

12. Seven

13. Nirvana

14. Chickens. There are BILLIONS more chickens in the world than there are humans.

15. Nine

Trivia Mix 9

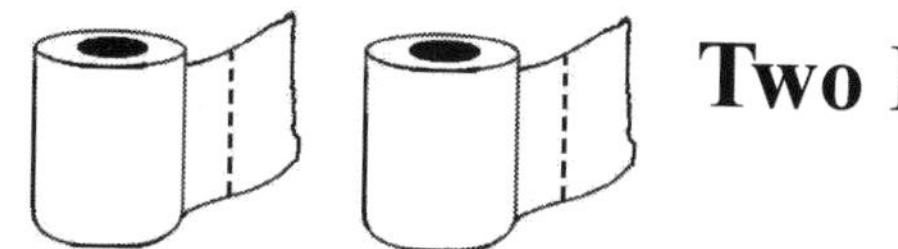

Two Rolls — Answers

1. Wrigley Field. The ballpark originally housed the Chicago Whales of the short-lived Federal League. In 1916, the Cubs moved in after the Federal League disbanded.

2. Generation

3. Pancreas

4. Ray Manzarek, John Densmore, and Robby Krieger

5. *Beavis and Butt-head*

6. Charles Lindbergh

7. Laks (or Lox)

8. Mount McKinley, or Denali

9. Quadrilateral

10. Boston Bruins, Chicago Blackhawks, Detroit Red Wings, Montreal Canadiens, New York Rangers, and Toronto Maple Leafs

11. *Quotations from Chairman Mao Zedong*, or *The Little Red Book*

12. David Frost's interviews were the subject of Frost/Nixon

13. Femur

14. The Andromeda Galaxy is closest to our Milky Way

15. Mongolian Empire. The British Empire of the early 1920s is considered by many to be slightly larger.

Trivia Mix 9

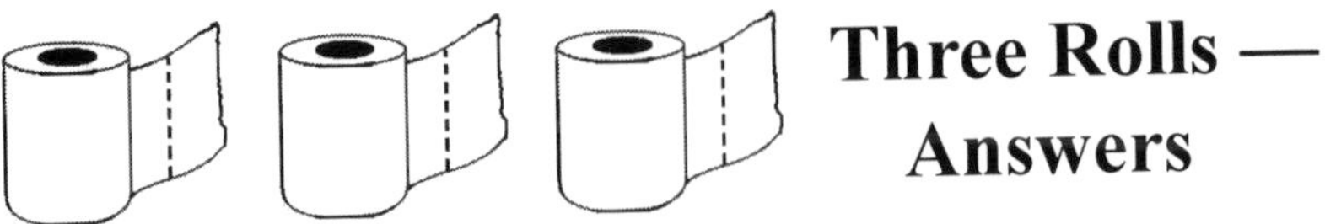

Three Rolls — Answers

1. Bob Dylan
2. Chukkas, Chukkers, or Chuckers
3. Charles Dow and Edward Jones
4. Megalodon
5. Ecuador
6. Sirius, Procyon, and Betelgeuse
7. Mel Tormé
8. Sophia
9. Ear wax
10. Beagle
11. *I Get Around* in 1964
12. Eight ounces
13. Antediluvian
14. Toyota Prius…he's concerned about the environment
15. The Jordanaires

Trivia Mix 10

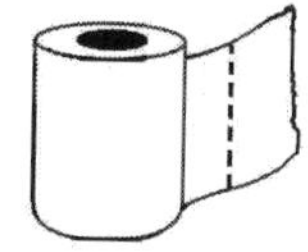

One Roll — Answers

1. The F1 key
2. Monticello
3. Jupiter
4. Bo
5. Pinocchio
6. Five
7. *Swish, swish, swish*
8. Alkaline batteries
9. Dijon mustard
10. Zamboni
11. Goodyear
12. Red
13. Doc Severinsen
14. Homophone
15. Georgia. It's also referred to as The Empire State of the South.

Trivia Mix 10

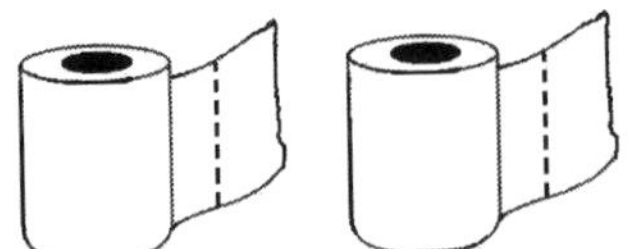

Two Rolls — Answers

1. Seven. Gilligan, the Skipper too, the Millionaire and his wife (the Howells), the movie star (Ginger), the Professor, and Mary Ann.

2. Bronx. Manhattan, Queens, Staten Island, and Brooklyn are either islands, or part of an island.

3. Gluteus maximus

4. Fusilli

5. Andrew Johnson and Bill Clinton

6. Gene Wilder and Johnny Depp

7. Mississippi River

8. Atmospheric pressure

9. Extra virgin olive oil. In 2007, EVOO was added to the Oxford American College Dictionary.

10. Marilyn Monroe

11. One Direction

12. John Steinbeck

13. 8-) or B-). Symbolic expressions like these are called emoticons.

14. *The Mole*

15. Pete Best

Trivia Mix 10

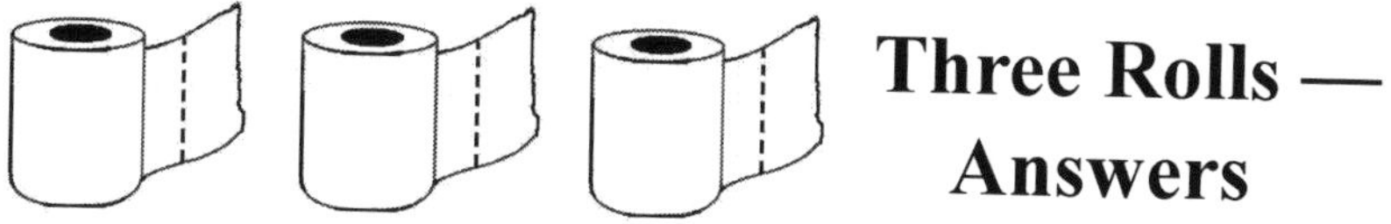

Three Rolls — Answers

1. Johnny Horton
2. Poison dart frog. Just a pin's head worth of toxin could bring down several elephants. Handle with care.
3. *Peek-A Who?*
4. Koosh ball
5. Utah
6. Archbishop of Canterbury
7. Andorra
8. Sam Snead recorded 82 wins. Tiger Woods is closing in as of 2013.
9. Twelve sides
10. SS *Andrea Doria*
11. The mud and debris flow that results from an eruption
12. The (John) Scopes Trial
13. Skin. Yes, skin is an organ.
14. Justin Guarini
15. All of these words have all 5 vowels in their spellings

Scorecard — Name: ____________________

Category	# Right		# of Pts.		Tot. Pts.
Trivia Mix 1 - 1 Roll		x	1	=	
Trivia Mix 1 - 2 Rolls		x	2	=	
Trivia Mix 1 - 3 Rolls		x	3	=	
Trivia Mix 2 - 1 Roll		x	1	=	
Trivia Mix 2 - 2 Rolls		x	2	=	
Trivia Mix 2 - 3 Rolls		x	3	=	
Trivia Mix 3 - 1 Roll		x	1	=	
Trivia Mix 3 - 2 Rolls		x	2	=	
Trivia Mix 3 - 3 Rolls		x	3	=	
Trivia Mix 4 - 1 Roll		x	1	=	
Trivia Mix 4 - 2 Rolls		x	2	=	
Trivia Mix 4 - 3 Rolls		x	3	=	
Trivia Mix 5 - 1 Roll		x	1	=	
Trivia Mix 5 - 2 Rolls		x	2	=	
Trivia Mix 5 - 3 Rolls		x	3	=	
Trivia Mix 6 - 1 Roll		x	1	=	
Trivia Mix 6 - 2 Rolls		x	2	=	
Trivia Mix 6 - 3 Rolls		x	3	=	
Trivia Mix 7 - 1 Roll		x	1	=	
Trivia Mix 7 - 2 Rolls		x	2	=	
Trivia Mix 7 - 3 Rolls		x	3	=	
Trivia Mix 8 - 1 Roll		x	1	=	
Trivia Mix 8 - 2 Rolls		x	2	=	
Trivia Mix 8 - 3 Rolls		x	3	=	
Trivia Mix 9 - 1 Roll		x	1	=	
Trivia Mix 9 - 2 Rolls		x	2	=	
Trivia Mix 9 - 3 Rolls		x	3	=	
Trivia Mix 10 - 1 Roll		x	1	=	
Trivia Mix 10 - 2 Rolls		x	2	=	
Trivia Mix 10 - 3 Rolls		x	3	=	

Grand Total

Scorecard — Name: ____________________

Category	# Right		# of Pts.		Tot. Pts.
Trivia Mix 1 - 1 Roll		x	1	=	
Trivia Mix 1 - 2 Rolls		x	2	=	
Trivia Mix 1 - 3 Rolls		x	3	=	
Trivia Mix 2 - 1 Roll		x	1	=	
Trivia Mix 2 - 2 Rolls		x	2	=	
Trivia Mix 2 - 3 Rolls		x	3	=	
Trivia Mix 3 - 1 Roll		x	1	=	
Trivia Mix 3 - 2 Rolls		x	2	=	
Trivia Mix 3 - 3 Rolls		x	3	=	
Trivia Mix 4 - 1 Roll		x	1	=	
Trivia Mix 4 - 2 Rolls		x	2	=	
Trivia Mix 4 - 3 Rolls		x	3	=	
Trivia Mix 5 - 1 Roll		x	1	=	
Trivia Mix 5 - 2 Rolls		x	2	=	
Trivia Mix 5 - 3 Rolls		x	3	=	
Trivia Mix 6 - 1 Roll		x	1	=	
Trivia Mix 6 - 2 Rolls		x	2	=	
Trivia Mix 6 - 3 Rolls		x	3	=	
Trivia Mix 7 - 1 Roll		x	1	=	
Trivia Mix 7 - 2 Rolls		x	2	=	
Trivia Mix 7 - 3 Rolls		x	3	=	
Trivia Mix 8 - 1 Roll		x	1	=	
Trivia Mix 8 - 2 Rolls		x	2	=	
Trivia Mix 8 - 3 Rolls		x	3	=	
Trivia Mix 9 - 1 Roll		x	1	=	
Trivia Mix 9 - 2 Rolls		x	2	=	
Trivia Mix 9 - 3 Rolls		x	3	=	
Trivia Mix 10 - 1 Roll		x	1	=	
Trivia Mix 10 - 2 Rolls		x	2	=	
Trivia Mix 10 - 3 Rolls		x	3	=	

Grand Total

Scorecard — Name: ____________________

Category	# Right		# of Pts.		Tot. Pts.
Trivia Mix 1 - 1 Roll		x	1	=	
Trivia Mix 1 - 2 Rolls		x	2	=	
Trivia Mix 1 - 3 Rolls		x	3	=	
Trivia Mix 2 - 1 Roll		x	1	=	
Trivia Mix 2 - 2 Rolls		x	2	=	
Trivia Mix 2 - 3 Rolls		x	3	=	
Trivia Mix 3 - 1 Roll		x	1	=	
Trivia Mix 3 - 2 Rolls		x	2	=	
Trivia Mix 3 - 3 Rolls		x	3	=	
Trivia Mix 4 - 1 Roll		x	1	=	
Trivia Mix 4 - 2 Rolls		x	2	=	
Trivia Mix 4 - 3 Rolls		x	3	=	
Trivia Mix 5 - 1 Roll		x	1	=	
Trivia Mix 5 - 2 Rolls		x	2	=	
Trivia Mix 5 - 3 Rolls		x	3	=	
Trivia Mix 6 - 1 Roll		x	1	=	
Trivia Mix 6 - 2 Rolls		x	2	=	
Trivia Mix 6 - 3 Rolls		x	3	=	
Trivia Mix 7 - 1 Roll		x	1	=	
Trivia Mix 7 - 2 Rolls		x	2	=	
Trivia Mix 7 - 3 Rolls		x	3	=	
Trivia Mix 8 - 1 Roll		x	1	=	
Trivia Mix 8 - 2 Rolls		x	2	=	
Trivia Mix 8 - 3 Rolls		x	3	=	
Trivia Mix 9 - 1 Roll		x	1	=	
Trivia Mix 9 - 2 Rolls		x	2	=	
Trivia Mix 9 - 3 Rolls		x	3	=	
Trivia Mix 10 - 1 Roll		x	1	=	
Trivia Mix 10 - 2 Rolls		x	2	=	
Trivia Mix 10 - 3 Rolls		x	3	=	

Grand Total

How did you do?

650 + — King/Queen of the Throne

600-649 — Topper of the Hopper

525-599 — Porcelain Prince/Princess

450-524 — Toileterrific!

375-449 — Keep Flushing for the Stars

300-374 — Might Need a Plunger

225-299 — Gotta call the Plumber

Below 225 — Clogged

Try a different Toiletrivia Book!

Made in the USA
Middletown, DE
13 December 2017